Cambridge BEC Vantage 2

WITH ANSWERS

Examination papers from University of Cambridge ESOL Examinations: English for Speakers of Other Languages

CAMBRIDGE
UNIVERSITY PRESS

CAMBRIDGE UNIVERSITY PRESS
Cambridge, New York, Melbourne, Madrid, Cape Town,
Singapore, São Paulo, Delhi, Tokyo, Mexico City

Cambridge University Press
The Edinburgh Building, Cambridge CB2 8RU, UK

Published in the United States of America by
Cambridge University Press, New York

www.cambridge.org
Information on this title: www.cambridge.org/9780521544542

First published 2004
6th printing 2011

A catalogue record for this publication is available from the British Library

ISBN 978-0-521-54454-2 Student's Book with answers
ISBN 978-0-521-54457-3 Audio Cassette
ISBN 978-0-521-54456-6 Set of 2 Audio CDs
ISBN 978-0-521-54455-9 Self-study Pack

ISBN 978-0-521-54454-2 Paperback

Contents

Statement of Results which includes a graphical display of their performance in each paper. These are shown against the scale Exceptional – Good – Borderline – Weak and indicate the candidate's relative performance in each paper.

TO THE TEACHER

Candidature

Each year BEC is taken by over 50,000 candidates throughout the world. Most candidates are either already in work or studying in preparation for the world of work.

Content, preparation and assessment

Material used throughout BEC is as far as possible authentic and free of bias, and reflects the international flavour of the examination. The subject matter should not advantage or disadvantage certain groups of candidates, nor should it offend in areas such as religion, politics or sex.

TEST OF READING

Part	Main Skill Focus	Input	Response	No. of questions
1	Reading – scanning and gist	One longer or four shorter informational texts (approx. 250–350 words in total)	Matching	7
2	Reading – understanding text structure	Single text: article, report, etc. with sentence-length gaps (text plus 7-option sentences approx. 450–550 words in total)	Matching	5
3	Reading for gist and specific information	Single text (approx. 450–550 words)	4-option multiple choice	6
4	Reading – vocabulary and structure information	Single informational text with lexical gaps (text including gapped words approx. 200–300 words)	4-option multiple choice cloze	15
5	Reading – understanding sentence structure / error identification	Short text (150–200 words) Identification of additional unnecessary words in text	Proof-reading	12

Reading Part One

This is a matching task. There are four short texts on a related theme (for example, descriptions of a group of products, or advertisements for jobs) or a single text divided into four sections. Although the context of each text will be similar, there will also be information that is particular to each text. The texts are labelled A–D. Candidates are presented with a set of seven items which are statements related to the texts. They are expected to match each statement with the relevant text. Questions in this part tend to focus mostly on the identification of specific information and detail. However, an item could focus on gist by testing areas such as the target reader or the topic.

Preparation

In order to prepare for this part it would be useful to familiarise students with sets of short texts that have a similar theme. Newspapers, magazines and catalogues are useful sources in which to find such texts. Students should be encouraged to look closely at all the information, particularly as short texts often include additional snippets of information on separate lines (such as prices, dates, titles, measurements, etc.) that can easily be overlooked.

Students could be set questions which test global reading skills prior to reading the texts, so that they are trained to think automatically of who a text is written for and why it has been written.

Reading Part Two

This is a matching task, comprising a text that has had six sentences removed from it and a set of seven sentences labelled A–G. Candidates are required to match each gap with the sentence which they think fits in terms of meaning and structure. The first gap is always given as an example so that candidates have five gaps left to complete. When they have finished this part there will be one sentence left which they have not used.

The texts for this part will have been chosen because they have a clear line of thought or argument that can still be discerned by the reader even with the sentences removed. When doing the task, therefore, students should be trained to read through the gapped text and the list of sentences first, in order to get an idea of what it is about. Having done that, they should be reassured that there is only one sentence that fits each gap.

This part is a test of text structure as well as meaning and the gaps will be reasonably far apart so that candidates can successfully anticipate the appropriate lexical and grammatical features of the missing sentence. Candidates can be expected to be tested on a variety of cohesive features with both a backward and forward reference, sometimes going beyond the sentence level. Thus, while selecting the appropriate sentence for a gap, they should read before and after the text to ensure that it fits well. At the end of this part, they should read through the entire text, inserting the gapped sentences as they go along, to ensure that the information is coherent.

Preparation

This can be quite a difficult task, especially for candidates who are unfamiliar with such an exercise. In preparing them for this part, it would be a good idea to select a number of graded texts that have clear, familiar ideas and evident cohesive features. Texts can be cut up, as they are in the test, or simply discussed in their entirety. In this way, students can work up to dealing with more complex material and identifying the many different ways that ideas are connected. It would also be useful when doing gapped texts to look at sentences that do not fit in gaps and discuss the reasons for this. Sometimes it is possible to make a sentence fit a gap by simply changing a few words. Discussion on areas such as this would also be fruitful.

Reading Part Three

This task consists of a text accompanied by four-option multiple choice items. The stem of a multiple choice item may take the form of a question or an incomplete sentence. There are six items, which are placed after the text. The text is 450 to 550 words long. Sources of original texts may be the general and business press, company literature, and books on topics such as management. Texts may be edited, but the source is authentic.

Preparation
- multiple choice questions are a familiar and long-standing type of test; here they are used to test opinion and inference rather than straightforward facts;
- correct answers are not designed to depend on simple word-matching, and students' ability to interpret paraphrasing should be developed;
- students should be encouraged to pursue their own interpretation of relevant parts of the text and then check their idea against the options offered, rather than reading all the options first;
- it could be useful for students to be given perhaps one of the wrong options only, and for them to try to write the correct answer and another wrong option.

Reading Part Four

This is a multiple choice cloze test with fifteen gaps, most of which test lexical items, and may focus on correct word choice, lexical collocations and fixed phrases. The texts chosen for this part will come from varied sources but they will all have a straightforward message or meaning, so that candidates are being tested on vocabulary and not on their comprehension of the passage.

Preparation
Candidates are usually familiar with this type of task and so it is most important to try and improve their range of vocabulary. The options provided in each item in the test will have similar meanings but only one word will be correct within the context provided. Familiarity with typical collocations would be especially useful. The language of business is often very precise and so it is worth spending time looking at the vocabulary used in different types of text, getting students to keep a vocabulary list and encouraging them to make active use of the lexical items that are new to them.

Reading Part Five

This is an error-correction or proof-reading task based on a text of 150 to 200 words, with twelve items. Candidates identify additional or unnecessary words in a text. This task can be related to the authentic task of checking a text for errors, and suitable text types are therefore letters, publicity materials, etc. The text is presented with twelve numbered lines, which are the lines containing the items. Further lines at the end may complete the text, but they are not numbered.

Preparation
- students should be reminded that this task represents a kind of editing that is common practice, even in their first language;
- any work on error analysis is likely to be helpful for this task;
- it may well be that photocopies of students' own writing could provide an authentic source for practice;
- a reverse of the exercise (giving students texts with missing words) might prove beneficial.

Marks

One mark is given for each correct answer. The total score is then weighted to 30 marks for the whole Reading paper.

TEST OF WRITING

Part	Functions/Communicative Task	Input	Response	Register
1	e.g. giving instructions, explaining a development, asking for comments, requesting information, agreeing to requests	Rubric only (plus layout of output text type)	Internal communication (medium may be note, message, memo or email) (40–50 words)	Neutral/ informal
2	Correspondence: e.g. explaining, apologising, reassuring, complaining Report: describing, summarising Proposal: describing, summarising, recommending, persuading	One or more pieces of input from: business correspondence (medium may be letter, fax or email), internal communication (medium may be note, memo or email), notice, advert, graphs, charts, etc. (plus layout if output is fax or email)	Business correspondence (medium may be letter or fax or email) or short report or proposal (medium may be memo or email) email (120–140 words)	Neutral/ formal

For BEC Vantage, candidates are required to produce two pieces of writing:
- an internal company communication; this means a piece of communication with a colleague or colleagues within the company on a business-related matter, and the delivery medium may be a note, message, memo or email;
- and one of the following:
  - a piece of business correspondence; this means correspondence with somebody outside the company (e.g. a customer or supplier) on a business-related matter, and the delivery medium may be a letter, fax or email;
  - a report; this means the presentation of information in relation to a specific issue or events. The report will contain an introduction, main body of findings and conclusion; it is possible that the delivery medium may be a memo or an email;
  - a proposal; this has a similar format to a report, but unlike the report, the focus of the proposal is on the future, with the main focus being on recommendations for discussion; it is possible that the delivery medium may be a memo or an email.

TEST OF LISTENING

Part	Main Skill Focus	Input	Response	No. of questions
1	Listening for writing short answers	Three telephone conversations or messages	Gap-filling	12
2	Listening; identifying topic, context, function, etc.	Short monologue; two sections of five 'snippets' each	Multiple matching	10
3	Listening	One extended conversation or monologue; interview, discussion, presentation, etc.	Multiple choice	8

Listening Part One

In this part, there are three conversations or answering machine messages, with a gapped text to go with each. Each gapped text provides a very clear context and has four spaces which have to be filled with one or two words or a number. The gapped texts may include forms, diary excerpts, invoices, message pads, etc. Candidates hear each conversation or message twice and as they listen they are required to complete the gapped text.

This part of the Listening test concentrates on the retrieval of factual information and it is important for candidates to listen carefully using the prompts on their question paper in order to identify the missing information. For example, they may have to note down a person's name, and if names on the tape are spelt out, those answers must be spelt correctly. Alternatively, they may have to listen for a room or telephone number, or an instruction or deadline. Answers to this part are rarely a simple matter of dictation and some reformulation of the prompt material will be required in order to locate the correct answer.

Listening Part Two

This part is divided into two sections. Each section has the same format: candidates hear five short monologues and have to match each monologue to a set of items, A–H. In each section, the eight options will form a coherent set and the overall theme or topic will be clearly stated in the task rubric. For example, candidates may hear five people talking and have to decide what sort of jobs the people do. Hence the set of options A–H will contain a list of jobs. Alternatively the set of options may consist of eight places/topics/addressees/purposes, etc. The two sections will always test different areas and so, if the first section focuses on, say, topics, the second section will focus on something else, such as functions.

In this part of the Listening test, candidates are being tested on their global listening skills and also on their ability to infer, extract gist and understand main ideas. In order to answer the questions successfully, they will need to work out the answer by developing ideas, and refining these as the text is heard. It will not be possible to 'word match' and candidates should not expect to hear such overt cues. However, there will always be a 'right' answer and candidates are not expected to opt for the 'best' answer.

Listening Part Three

A longer text is heard in this part, usually lasting approximately four minutes. The text will typically be an interview, conversation or discussion with two or more speakers, or possibly a presentation or report with one speaker. There are eight, three-option multiple choice questions that focus on details and main ideas in the text. There may be questions on opinions and feelings but these will be relatively straightforward and will not require candidates to remember long or complex pieces of information.

Preparing for the Listening paper

All listening practice should be helpful for students, whether authentic or specially prepared. In particular, discussion should focus on:
- the purpose of speeches and conversations or discussions
- the speakers' role
- the opinions expressed
- the language functions employed
- relevant aspects of phonology such as stress, linking and weak forms, etc.
  In addition, students should be encouraged to appreciate the differing demands of each task type. It will be helpful not only to practise the task types in order to develop a sense of familiarity and confidence, but also to discuss how the three task types relate to real-life skills and situations:
- the first is note-taking (and therefore productive), and students should reflect on the various situations in which they take notes from a spoken input; they should also be encouraged to try to predict the kinds of words or numbers that might go in the gaps
- the second is a matching (with discrimination) exercise, and reflects the ability to interrelate information between reading and listening and across differing styles and registers
- the third involves the correct interpretation of spoken input, with correct answers often being delivered across different speakers.
  In all three tasks, successful listening depends on correct reading, and students should be encouraged to make full use of the pauses during the test to check the written input.

Marks

One mark is given for each correct answer, giving a total score of 30 marks for the whole Listening paper.

TEST OF SPEAKING

Part	Format/Content	Time	Interaction Focus
1	Conversation between the interlocutor and each candidate Giving personal information. Talking about present circumstances, past experiences and future plans, expressing opinions, speculating, etc.	About 3 minutes	The interlocutor encourages the candidates to give information about themselves and to express personal opinions
2	A 'mini presentation' by each candidate on a business theme Organising a larger unit of discourse. Giving information and expressing and justifying opinions	About 6 minutes	The candidates are given prompts which generate a short talk on a business-related topic
3	Two-way conversation between candidates followed by further prompting from the interlocutor. Expressing and justifying opinions, speculating, comparing and contrasting, agreeing and disagreeing, etc.	About 5 minutes	The candidates are presented with a discussion on a business-related topic The interlocutor extends the discussion with prompts on related topics

The Speaking test is conducted by two oral examiners (an interlocutor and an assessor), with pairs of candidates. The interlocutor is responsible for conducting the Speaking test and is also required to give a mark for each candidate's performance during the whole test. The assessor is responsible for providing an analytical assessment of each candidate's performance and, after being introduced by the interlocutor, takes no further part in the interaction.

The Speaking test is designed for pairs of candidates. However, where a centre has an uneven number of candidates, the last three candidates will be examined together. Oral examiner packs contain shared tasks which are particularly appropriate for these groups of three.

Speaking Part One

In the first part of the test, the interlocutor addresses each candidate in turn and asks first general, then more business-related questions. Candidates will not be addressed in strict sequence. This part of the test lasts about three minutes and during this time candidates are being tested on their ability to talk briefly about themselves, and to perform functions such as agreeing and disagreeing, and expressing preferences.

Speaking Part Two

The second part of the test is a 'mini presentation'. In this part, the candidates are given a choice of topic and have a minute to prepare a piece of extended speech lasting approximately one minute. After each candidate has spoken their partner is invited to ask a question about what has been said.

Speaking Part Three

The third part of the test is a two-way conversation (three-way in a three-candidate format) between candidates. The interlocutor gives candidates a topic to discuss. The candidates are asked to speak for about three minutes. The interlocutor will support the conversation as appropriate and then ask further questions related to the main theme.

Preparing for the Speaking test

It is important to familiarise candidates with the format of the test before it takes place, by the use of paired activities in class. Teachers may need to explain the benefits of this type of assessment to candidates. The primary purpose of paired assessment is to sample a wider range of discourse than can be elicited from an individual interview. In the first part of the test, candidates mainly respond to questions or comments from the interlocutor.

Students need practice in exchanging personal and non-personal information; at Vantage level it may be possible for students to practise talking about themselves in pairs with or without prompts (such as written questions). However, prompt materials are necessary for Parts Two and Three, and students could be encouraged to design these themselves or may be provided with specially prepared sets. In small classes, students could discuss authentic materials as a group prior to engaging in pairwork activities. Such activities familiarise students with the types of interactive skills involved in asking and providing factual information, such as: speaking clearly, formulating questions, listening carefully and giving precise answers.

In the 'mini presentation', candidates are being asked to show an ability to talk for an extended period of time. Discussion activities as well as giving short talks or presentations should help to develop this skill.

In the final discussion in the Vantage Speaking test, candidates are also being tested on their ability to express opinions, to compare and contrast, to concede points and possibly to reach a conclusion (although it is perfectly acceptable for candidates to agree to differ). Any discussion activities on a business theme that encourage students to employ these skills will be beneficial. Group or class discussions are valuable ways of developing these skills.

Assessment

Candidates are assessed on their own performance and not in relation to each other according to the following analytical criteria; Grammar and Vocabulary, Discourse Management, Pronunciation and Interactive Communication. These criteria are interpreted at Vantage level. Assessment is based on performance in the whole test and is not related to particular parts of the test.

Both examiners assess the candidates. The assessor applies detailed, analytical scales, and the interlocutor applies a Global Achievement Scale which is based on the analytical scales. The analytical criteria are further described below:

Grammar and Vocabulary

This refers to range and accuracy as well as the appropriate use of grammatical and lexical forms. At BEC Vantage level, a range of grammar and vocabulary is

Test 1

READING   1 hour

PART ONE

Questions 1–7

- Look at the statements below and the text on the opposite page about the use of coaching in staff development.
- Which section (**A**, **B**, **C** or **D**) does each statement (**1–7**) refer to?
- For each statement (**1–7**), mark one letter (**A**, **B**, **C** or **D**) on your Answer Sheet.
- You will need to use some of these letters more than once.

Example:

0 the best coaches being committed to their work and feeling pleased with what they achieve

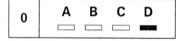

---

1 the contact between coach and employee not solving all difficulties at work

2 the discussion of how certain situations could be better handled if they occur again

3 a coach encouraging an employee to apply what has been taught to routine work situations

4 coaching providing new interest to individuals who are unhappy in their current positions

5 coaching providing a supportive environment to discuss performance

6 employees being asked to analyse themselves and practise greater self-awareness

7 coaching enabling a company to respond rapidly to a lack of expertise in a certain area

Coaching

A

Coaching involves two or more people sitting down together to talk through issues that have come up recently at work, and analysing how they were managed and how they might be dealt with more effectively on subsequent occasions. Coaching thus transfers skills and information from one person to another in an on-the-job situation so that the work experience of the coach is used to advise and guide the individual being coached. It also allows successes and failures to be evaluated in a non-threatening atmosphere.

B

Coaching means influencing the learner's personal development, for example his or her confidence and ambition. It can take place any time during an individual's career. Coaching is intended to assist individuals to function more effectively, and it is a powerful learning model. It begins where skills-based training ends, and helps individuals to use formally learnt knowledge in day-to-day work and management situations. Individuals being coached are in a demanding situation with their coach, which requires them to consider their own behaviour and question their reasons for doing things.

C

The coach professionally assists the career development of another individual, outside the normal manager/subordinate relationship. In theory, the coaching relationship should provide answers to every problem, but in practice it falls short of this. However, it can provide a space for discussion and feedback on topics such as people management and skills, behaviour patterns, confidence-building and time management. Through coaching, an organisation can meet skills shortages, discuss targets and indicate how employees should deal with challenging situations, all at short notice.

D

Effective coaches are usually those who get satisfaction from the success of others and who give time to the coaching role. Giving people coaching responsibilities can support their development, either by encouraging management potential through small-scale one-to-one assignments, or by providing added job satisfaction to managers who feel they are stuck in their present jobs. A coach is also a confidential adviser, accustomed to developing positive and effective approaches to complex management, organisational and change problems.

PART TWO

Questions 8–12

- Read the article below about a catering company.
- Choose the best sentence from the opposite page to fill each of the gaps.
- For each gap (**8–12**), mark one letter (**A–G**) on your Answer Sheet.
- Do not use any letter more than once.
- There is an example at the beginning, (**0**).

BUFFET ZONE

Lucy Robertson started working at a take-away food business to supplement her income during her student days at Edinburgh University. Several years later she had bought the business and now, 17 years on, she owns Grapevine Caterers, probably Scotland's leading independent caterers, with a turnover of almost £6m.

She had never planned to own a business, and had certainly never considered a career in catering. (**0**) ....*G*.... . However, her unplanned career began in 1985, when she returned to Edinburgh and discovered that the takeaway she had worked in was up for sale. On impulse, she bought it, but admits that at the time she knew nothing about catering. (**8**) .... It was a difficult time, but essential in terms of gaining the experience she needed. The late 1980s boom was good for business, with large numbers of office workers wanting takeaway food for their lunches. (**9**) .... 'At one point there were 26 food outlets within a 5-kilometre radius,' Robertson recalls. As the economy changed and the once packed office blocks started to become vacant, it became clear that Robertson would need to diversify. (**10**) .... It changed the direction of the company for good.

As Robertson began to win catering contracts, she decided that the company would have to move to larger premises. In 1994, the move was made when she bought another catering business that already had a number of profitable contracts for boardroom lunches.

Meanwhile, Robertson's main competitor, the oldest catering company in Edinburgh, was causing her some anxiety. 'Customer loyalty is not to be underestimated,' she warns. But Robertson is not someone who is easily put off. (**11**) .... Partly as a result of this, turnover doubled, and having outgrown another site, Robertson bought a city-centre location for the group's headquarters.

By now, Grapevine's main competitor was a new catering company called Towngates. Although Robertson tried to raise enough money to buy Towngates, she did not succeed. Then luck intervened and Towngates went bankrupt. (**12**) .... Many accepted and the company's turnover went from £700,000 to £1.5 million almost overnight.

However, the company's growth was not as smooth as it sounds in retrospect. Robertson admits, 'We were close to the edge during the growth period. Like many under-capitalised companies trying to grow, it might easily have collapsed.' But that, she feels, is the challenge of developing your own business.

Example:

0	A	B	C	D	E	F	G
	☐	☐	☐	☐	☐	☐	▬

A But there are plenty of similar contracts to be won in the east of Scotland before Robertson turns her attention elsewhere.

B Her way round this particular problem was to recruit the catering manager of the rival company.

C But this demand was short-lived, and before long, increasing competition made it harder to make a profit.

D 'It was a dramatic learning curve and very small amounts of money were earned at first,' says Robertson.

E She decided that the solution, since many companies required working lunches for meetings with clients, was to prepare and deliver meals to business premises.

F On hearing this, Robertson immediately contacted all of their clients and offered the services of Grapevine Caterers.

G Instead, she studied accountancy after leaving university, and a steady if unspectacular professional path seemed set.

PART THREE

Questions 13–18

- Read the article below about an image consultant who advises people on how to present themselves in the world of work, and the questions on the opposite page.
- For each question (**13–18**), mark one letter (**A**, **B**, **C** or **D**) on your Answer Sheet.

HOW TO MARKET YOURSELF

We manage our own careers now. So knowing how to brand and position yourself in the market as 'Me plc' at different stages of your working life is becoming an increasingly vital skill. At least that is what image expert Mary Spillane believes. 'Employment as we know it is decreasing. Jobs don't exist, work exists. In the next decade most of us will be suppliers, not staff. We will have clients not bosses. If you are under 30, you probably know that there is only one firm to join for life: Me plc. It promotes you and your potential to others.'

'We're working in multi-national, multi-cultural, multi-corporate teams and it's important to understand the implications of this. We need to create a personal brand that is unique, but complements the brand of the corporation we are working for. You have to find a way to do it so that you are not just a typical employee,' advises Spillane. 'You have to decide what central values you want to project, and also what may need to alter from situation to situation.'

Many people only remember Mary Spillane for the years she spent running a cosmetics company, but she actually has masters degrees in information science and politics. She used to hide that hard-hitting side, but is now eager to show it and forget about cosmetics. 'Now that I'm working in the boardrooms of major plcs and global companies, I'm playing up my degrees and management background so that the image side is seen only as an addition to the value side,' says Spillane.

Some contracts take longer than others. 'The City law firms I'm currently working for are really difficult because they don't have any idea of what their brand should be, and are still very

traditional even when talking about becoming modern. I'm showing them how to do everything from changing their reception areas – which tend to be very off-putting with their high-fronted reception desks – to how to make small talk that is less formal and rigid. Companies rebrand themselves all the time, spending millions on new office interiors and so on. But without an underlying change of attitudes, it can prove an empty exercise.'

She argues that for individuals too, there must be more than a surface change, as rebranding goes deeper than a mere change of wardrobe. Beyond advice on appearance, she tells clients, 'Remind yourself of what you are selling: the personal values that comprise your brand. Learn to present yourself in a way that will project what you want to deliver. Lifelong learning is essential, together with the sort of discovery and adventure that promote personal growth. Always have an up-to-the-minute CV ready to print out, refreshing it every few months with your most recent achievements, just to remind others of your brand value.'

She believes it is essential that you understand both your public self and your private self, as well as your blind spots and your potential, in order to create an effective brand. 'The public self is the image you project to the world, the private self is what you know about yourself but others don't, and blind spots are those things that others see about you but you can't see for yourself. By deciding what image you want other people to see, emphasising more of your private self and sorting out a few blind spots, you will increase not only your potential to influence others, but also your self-esteem and self-confidence.'

13 In the first paragraph, Mary Spillane says people should learn how to market themselves because

    A   it encourages companies to give them a job for life.
    B   in the future it will be a company requirement.
    C   in many careers it is becoming difficult to succeed.
    D   it will help them adapt to developments in the job market.

14 Spillane says that, when creating a personal brand, it is important to

    A   change things depending on the circumstances.
    B   decide what image people would like you to present.
    C   make sure that colleagues feel at ease with your image.
    D   follow the example of someone in the company you work for.

15 What do we learn about Spillane in the third paragraph?

    A   She is embarrassed about her career with a cosmetics company.
    B   She doesn't like talking about her academic background.
    C   She has qualifications many people are unaware of.
    D   She worries about how other people see her.

16 Which problem does Spillane refer to when talking about the companies she is presently working with?

    A   They find it difficult to accept her ideas.
    B   They are unaware of how to rebrand themselves.
    C   They don't want to spend large amounts of money.
    D   They are unwilling to modernise their work environment.

17 When advising people on rebranding themselves, Spillane tells them to

    A   attend courses to gain specialist skills.
    B   update regularly their written proof of what they can do.
    C   try out different ways of presenting themselves to others.
    D   remember that what they look like is the most important point.

18 Spillane says that, in order to rebrand yourself successfully, it is important to

    A   ask for other people's opinions about your image.
    B   feel confident about what you are trying to achieve.
    C   learn how to make use of all aspects of your character.
    D   model yourself on people with a certain amount of influence.

PART FOUR

Questions 19–33

- Read the text below about planning.
- Choose the best word or phrase to fill each gap from **A**, **B**, **C** or **D** on the opposite page.
- For each question (**19–33**), mark one letter (**A**, **B**, **C** or **D**) on your Answer Sheet.
- There is an example at the beginning, (**0**).

Planning

In any planning system, from the simplest budgeting to the most complex corporate planning, there is an annual (**0**) ....Ç... . This is partly due to the fact that firms (**19**) .... their accounting on a yearly (**20**) .... , but also because similar (**21**) .... often occur in the market.

Usually, the larger the firm, the longer the planning takes. But typically, planning for next year may start nine months or more in advance, with various stages of evaluation leading to (**22**) .... of the complete plan three months before the start of the year.

Planning continues, however, throughout the year, since managers (**23**) .... progress against targets, while looking forward to the next year. What is happening now will (**24**) .... the objectives and plans for the future.

In today's business climate, as markets constantly change and become more difficult to (**25**) .... , some analysts believe that long-term planning is pointless. In some markets they may be right, as long as companies can build the sort of flexibility into their (**26**) .... which allows them to (**27**) .... to any sudden changes.

Most firms, however, need to plan more than one year ahead in order to (**28**) .... their long-term goals. This may reflect the time it takes to commission and build a new production plant, or, in marketing (**29**) .... , it may be a question of how long it takes to research and launch a range of new products, and reach a certain (**30**) .... in the market. If, for example, it is going to take five years for a particular airline to become the (**31**) .... choice amongst business travellers on certain routes, the airline must plan for the various (**32**) .... involved.

Every one-year plan, therefore, must be (**33**) .... in relation to longer-term plans, and it should contain the stages that are necessary to achieve the final goals.

Example:

A performance   **B** transaction   **C** process   **D** action

0	A	B	C	D
	☐	☐	■	☐

19	**A** make up	**B** carry out	**C** bring about	**D** put down
20	**A** basis	**B** grounds	**C** foundation	**D** structure
21	**A** distributions	**B** guides	**C** designs	**D** patterns
22	**A** approval	**B** permission	**C** consent	**D** decision
23	**A** value	**B** inspect	**C** review	**D** survey
24	**A** command	**B** prompt	**C** influence	**D** persuade
25	**A** guess	**B** speculate	**C** reckon	**D** predict
26	**A** operations	**B** techniques	**C** measures	**D** exercises
27	**A** answer	**B** respond	**C** counter	**D** reply
28	**A** move	**B** lead	**C** develop	**D** benefit
29	**A** expressions	**B** descriptions	**C** words	**D** terms
30	**A** reputation	**B** position	**C** situation	**D** influence
31	**A** desired	**B** selected	**C** preferred	**D** supposed
32	**A** acts	**B** steps	**C** means	**D** points
33	**A** handed over	**B** drawn up	**C** made out	**D** written off

PART TWO

- You work in the Customer Services Department of a mail-order company. You have been asked to prepare a short report for your line manager about complaints.
- Look at the information below, on which you have already made some handwritten notes.
- Then, using **all** your handwritten notes, write your **report**.
- Write **120–140** words.

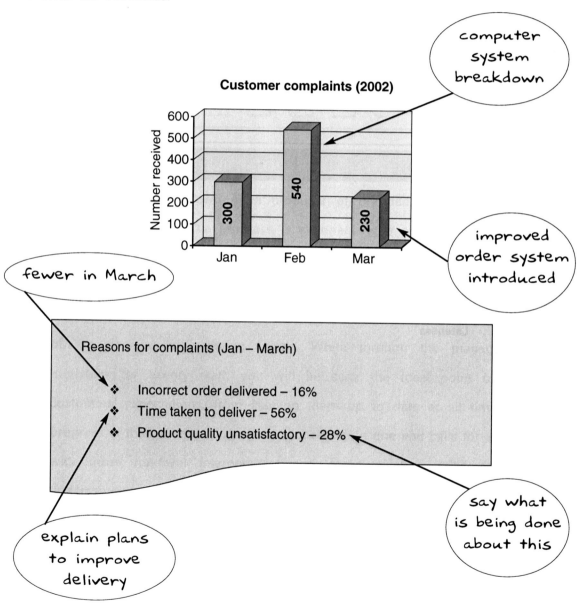

LISTENING   40 minutes (including 10 minutes' transfer time)

PART ONE

Questions 1–12

- You will hear three telephone conversations or messages.
- Write **one** or **two** words or a number in the numbered spaces on the notes or forms below.
- After you have listened once, replay each recording.

Conversation One

(Questions 1–4)

- Look at the form below.
- You will hear a man asking a colleague for information about a former employee.

Personnel Record

NAME:	Stephen (1) ....
ADDRESS:	183 School Road, Barnfield, BF2 8TP
DEPARTMENT:	(2) ....
POST HELD:	(3) .... (temporary)
MONTHLY SALARY:	(4) £ ....

Conversation Two

(Questions 5–8)

- Look at the note below.
- You will hear a man describing a problem with an order.

WHILE YOU WERE OUT

Message for: Steven Kirby

From: Mark Jones

Company: (5) ....

Message

Re: Stationery order

Problem with the (6) .... ordered.

The (7) .... need 500 and he needs 750.

Also (8) .... needs to be repositioned.

Conversation Three

(Questions 9–12)

- Look at the notes below.
- You will hear a woman making the arrangements for a delegation who are going to visit her company.

Delegation visit – things to do

Prepare an (9) .... for each delegate.

Book 1pm lunch at (10) ....

Meet delegates when they arrive
at the (11) .... ,

Show them the (12) .... first.

PART TWO

Questions 13–22

Section One

(Questions 13–17)

- You will hear five short recordings.
- For each recording, decide which type of document the speaker is talking about.
- Write one letter (**A–H**) next to the number of the recording.
- Do not use any letter more than once.
- After you have listened once, replay the recordings.

13 ....

14 ....

15 ....

16 ....

17 ....

A	an invoice
B	a price-list
C	a bank statement
D	a receipt
E	a company cheque
F	a balance sheet
G	a contract
H	an expenses claim form

Section Two

(Questions 18–22)

- You will hear another five recordings.
- For each recording, decide what the speaker's purpose is.
- Write one letter (**A–H**) next to the number of the recording.
- Do not use any letter more than once.
- After you have listened once, replay the recordings.

18 ....

19 ....

20 ....

21 ....

22 ....

A	to make a complaint
B	to deny something
C	to offer assistance
D	to ask for advice
E	to express doubt
F	to ask for permission
G	to explain an action
H	to recommend a new policy

PART THREE

Questions 23–30

- You will hear the chairman of a business institute making a speech about new business awards that his institute has sponsored.
- For each question (**23–30**), mark one letter (**A, B** or **C**) for the correct answer.
- After you have listened once, replay the recording.

23   The aim of the 'Business Today' competition was to reward

    A   good product design.
    B   skilful project management.
    C   rapid financial success.

24   How many companies were chosen to compete in the final of the competition?

    A   four
    B   fourteen
    C   forty

25   The types of products which the finalists were developing

    A   caused considerable problems for the judges.
    B   were all connected with the food industry.
    C   involved a common set of development aspects.

26   According to the speaker, what are small firms good at?

    A   fitting new products in with current production
    B   recording methods used in developing new products
    C   developing new management structures for new products

27   The speaker believes big companies document innovation well because of

    A   the number of staff available.
    B   the involvement of senior management.
    C   the insistence on regular procedures.

28   The panel was impressed by Natura because they had

    A   invested considerable time inventing a new product.
    B   researched new ways of manufacturing their product.
    C   investigated new overseas markets for their product.

29 The judges praised the links between development teams in smaller companies and

    A   senior management.
    B   suppliers.
    C   the market.

30 The companies sometimes had problems because the suppliers

    A   could not understand the specifications.
    B   could not meet the deadlines.
    C   could not rely on their subcontractors.

You now have 10 minutes to transfer your answers to your Answer Sheet.

SPEAKING   14 minutes

SAMPLE SPEAKING TASKS

PART ONE

The interview – about 3 minutes

In this part the interlocutor asks questions to each of the candidates in turn. You have to give information about yourself and express personal opinions.

PART TWO

'Mini presentation' – about 6 minutes

In this part of the test you are asked to give a short talk on a business topic. You have to choose one of the topics from the three below and then talk for about one minute. You have one minute to prepare your ideas.

A   WHAT IS IMPORTANT WHEN ...?

Entertaining clients
- Types of activities
- Cost
-
-

B   WHAT IS IMPORTANT WHEN ...?

Choosing retail premises to rent
- Location
- Length of contract
-
-

C   WHAT IS IMPORTANT WHEN ...?

Deciding on packaging for products
- Image
- Production process
-
-

PART THREE

Discussion – about 5 minutes

In this part of the test you are given a discussion topic. You have **30** seconds to look at the prompt card, an example of which is below, and then about three minutes to discuss the topic with your partner. After that the examiner will ask you more questions related to the topic.

For **two** candidates

> **Work Experience Programme**
>
> The manufacturing company you work for has decided to offer a two-week work experience programme for a small group of students from a local business college.
>
> You have been asked to help with the preparations for this programme.
>
> Discuss the situation together, and decide:
>
> - what kinds of work experience the company might offer
>
> - how the participants should be selected.

For **three** candidates

> **Work Experience Programme**
>
> The manufacturing company you work for has decided to offer a two-week work experience programme for a small group of students from a local business college.
>
> You have been asked to help with the preparations for this programme.
>
> Discuss the situation together, and decide:
>
> - what kinds of work experience the company might offer
>
> - how the participants should be selected
>
> - what feedback and evaluation should take place after the programme has finished.

Follow-on questions

- What other preparations would the company need to make before receiving work experience students? (Why?)

- What are the advantages to a company of offering a work experience programme to business students? (Why?)

- What do you think is the most useful kind of work experience for business students? (Why?)

- What help would you give a student on their first day of work experience? (Why?)

- Which areas of business would you like to have more experience of? (Why?)

- In what ways can businesses develop close links with the community?

PART TWO

Questions 8–12

- Read the article below about recruiting staff.
- Choose the best sentence from the opposite page to fill each of the gaps.
- For each gap (**8–12**), mark one letter (**A–G**) on your Answer Sheet.
- Do not use any letter more than once.
- There is an example at the beginning, (**0**).

Finding the right people

When a small company grows, managers must take on many new roles. Besides the day-to-day running of the business, they find themselves responsible for, among other things, relations with outside investors, increased levels of cashflow and, hardest of all, recruitment.

For most managers of small and medium-sized enterprises, the job of searching for, interviewing and selecting staff is difficult and time-consuming. (**0**) ...*G*... . Interviewing, for example, is a highly skilled activity in itself.

'We have found the whole process very hard,' says Dan Baker, founding partner of a PR company. 'In seven years we have grown from five to eighteen staff, but we have not found it easy to locate and recruit the right people.' (**8**) .... As Dan Baker explains, 'We went to one for our first recruitment drive, but they took a lot of money in advance and didn't put forward anybody suitable. In the end we had to do it ourselves.'

Most recruitment decisions are based on a pile of CVs, a couple of short interviews and two cautious references. David Rowe, a business psychologist, studied how appointments were made in five small companies. He claims that selection was rarely based on clear criteria. (**9**) .... This kind of approach to recruitment often has unhappy consequences for both employers and new recruits.

Small companies often know what kind of person they are looking for. (**10**) .... According to David Rowe, this means that small company managers themselves have to devote more time and energy to recruitment. It shouldn't be something that is left to the evenings or weekends.

Many companies start the recruitment process with over-optimistic ideas about the type of person that will fit into their team. 'It's very easy to say you must have the best people in the top positions,' says Alex Jones, managing partner of an executive recruitment company. 'But someone who is excellent in one company may not do so well in another environment. (**11**) .... You can never guarantee a successful transfer of skills.'

Whatever the candidate's qualifications, their personal qualities are just as important since they will have to integrate with existing members of staff. This is where, the recruitment industry argues, they can really help.

According to Alex Jones, 'A good recruitment agency will visit your company and ask a lot of questions. (**12**) .... They can ask applicants all sorts of questions you don't like to ask and present you with a shortlist of people who not only have the skills, but who are likely to fit in with your company's way of doing things.'

Example:

A A finance director in a big company, for example, will often make a terrible small company finance director because he or she is used to having a team doing the day-to-day jobs.

B More often than not, the people making the choice prioritised different qualities in candidates or relied on guesswork.

C Recruitment would seem an obvious task to outsource, but the company's experience of recruitment agencies was not encouraging.

D They need paying for that, of course, but you will have them working for you and not for the candidate.

E They are usually in very specific markets and the problem they face is that recruitment agencies may not really understand the sector.

F This means that companies cannot spend more than the standard ten minutes interviewing each applicant.

G Yet few are trained and competent for all aspects of the task.

PART THREE

Questions 13–18

- Read the article below about Smithson's, a British department store, and the questions on the opposite page.
- For each question (**13–18**), mark one letter (**A, B, C** or **D**) on your Answer Sheet.

Department Store Magic

For most of the 20th century Smithson's was one of Britain's most successful department stores, but by the mid-1990s, it had become dull. Still profitable, thanks largely to a series of successful advertising campaigns, but decidedly boring. The famous were careful not to be seen there, and its sales staff didn't seem to have changed since the store opened in 1908. Worst of all, its customers were buying fewer and fewer of its own-brand products, the major part of its business, and showing a preference for more fashionable brands.

But now all this has changed, thanks to Rowena Baker, who became Smithson's first woman Chief Executive three years ago. Since then, while most major retailers in Britain have been losing money, Smithson's profits have been rising steadily. When Baker started, a lot of improvements had just been made to the building, without having any effect on sales, and she took the bold decision to invite one of Europe's most exciting interior designers to develop the fashion area, the heart of the store. This very quickly led to rising sales, even before the goods on display were changed. And as sales grew, so did profits.

Baker had ambitious plans for the store from the start. 'We're playing a big game, to prove we're up there with the leaders in our sector, and we have to make sure people get that message. Smithson's had fallen behind the competition. It provided a traditional service targeted at middle-aged, middle-income customers, who'd been shopping there for years, and the customer base was gradually contracting. Our idea is to sell such an exciting variety of goods that everyone will want to come in, whether they plan to spend a little or a lot.' Baker's vision for the store is clear, but achieving it is far from simple. At first, many employees resisted her improvements because they just wouldn't be persuaded that there was anything wrong with the way they'd always done things, even if they accepted that the store had to overtake its competitors. It took many long meetings, involving the entire workforce, to win their support. It helped when they realised that Baker was a very different kind of manager from the ones they had known.

Baker's staff policies contained more surprises. The uniform that had hardly changed since day one has now disappeared. Moreover, teenagers now get young shop assistants, and staff in the sports departments are themselves sports fans in trainers. As Baker explains, 'How can you sell jeans if you're wearing a black suit? Smithson's has a new identity, and this needs to be made clear to the customers.' She's also given every sales assistant responsibility for ensuring customer satisfaction, even if it means occasionally breaking company rules in the hope that this will help company profits.

Rowena Baker is proving successful, but the City's big investors haven't been persuaded. According to retail analyst, John Matthews, 'Money had already been invested in refurbishment of the store and in fact that led to the boost in sales. She took the credit, but hadn't done anything to achieve it. And in my view the company's shareholders are not convinced. The fact is that unless she opens several more stores pretty soon, Smithson's profits will start to fall because turnover at the existing store will inevitably start to decline.'

13 According to the writer, in the mid-1990s Smithson's department store

  A was making a loss.
  B had a problem keeping staff.
  C was unhappy with its advertising agency.
  D mostly sold goods under the Smithson's name.

14 According to the writer, Smithson's profits started rising three years ago because of

  A an improvement in the retailing sector.
  B the previous work done on the store.
  C Rowena Baker's choice of designer.
  D a change in the products on sale.

15 According to Rowena Baker, one problem which Smithson's faced when she joined was that

  A the number of people using the store was falling slowly.
  B its competitors offered a more specialised range of products.
  C the store's prices were set at the wrong level.
  D customers were unhappy with the service provided.

16 According to the writer, many staff opposed Baker's plans because

  A they were unwilling to change their way of working.
  B they disagreed with her goals for the store.
  C they felt they were not consulted enough about the changes.
  D they were unhappy with her style of management.

17 Baker has changed staff policies because she believes that

  A the corporate image can be improved through staff uniforms.
  B the previous rules were not fair to customers.
  C customers should be able to identify with the staff serving them.
  D employees should share in company profits.

18 What problem does John Matthews think Smithson's is facing?

  A More money needs to be invested in the present store.
  B The company's profits will only continue to rise if it expands.
  C The refurbishment of the store is proving unpopular with customers.
  D Smithson's shareholders expect a quick return on their investments.

PART FOUR

Questions 19–33

- Read the introduction below to a book about relationships at work.
- Choose the best word to fill each gap from **A, B, C** or **D** on the opposite page.
- For each question (**19–33**), mark one letter (**A, B, C** or **D**) on your Answer Sheet.
- There is an example at the beginning, (**0**).

MANAGING UPWARDS

Managing a career on the way up is quite different from managing one at the (**0**) ...ᶜ... of an organisation. Individuals on the way up have to build relationships with the people they (**19**) .... to. They usually have to (**20**) .... with subordinates in addition to people at the same level as themselves. The most senior staff only have those under them to relate to. This book (**21**) .... the idea that all working relationships, including the relationship with one's boss, can and should be managed.

You do not have to be (**22**) .... than your manager in order to manage the relationship. Nor do you have to be better than your manager in any (**23**) .... Your manager may well be your career (**24**) .... and guide: he or she may have taught you almost everything you know about your (**25**) .... of business – and may continue to teach you more. You may be planning to remain under his or her guidance in the future. None of these (**26**) .... should alter your relationship with your manager or (**27**) .... you off 'managing upwards'. I use this phrase to (**28**) .... to the management of one's boss because, for many people on the way up, it is the first relationship they have to get right.

You can, of course, get on at work just by (**29**) .... positively to your manager, but that is not likely to be the most successful way to (**30**) .... your working life. An active policy of managing upwards will make you more successful and, at the same time, make the business of going to work more enjoyable. It can also be a way to show (**31**) .... to your manager for the efforts he or she has made on your (**32**) .... Finally, managing upwards will make it easier for your manager to manage you, leaving him or her more time for other (**33**) .... and tasks.

Example:

A height	B peak	C point	D top

0	A ☐	B ☐	C ☐	D ▬

19	A notify	B inform	C account	D report
20	A unite	B contact	C handle	D deal
21	A promotes	B presses	C advertises	D convinces
22	A clearer	B deeper	C smarter	D fuller
23	A respect	B fashion	C part	D means
24	A leader	B supporter	C adviser	D helper
25	A course	B line	C path	D route
26	A factors	B aspects	C causes	D topics
27	A put	B see	C keep	D take
28	A specify	B identify	C indicate	D refer
29	A giving	B operating	C reacting	D co-operating
30	A run	B forward	C move	D make
31	A appraisal	B value	C appreciation	D regard
32	A advantage	B benefit	C side	D behalf
33	A posts	B roles	C positions	D acts

PART FIVE

Questions 34–45

- Read the article below about the winner of a business award.
- In most of the lines (**34–45**) there is one extra word. It is either grammatically incorrect or does not fit in with the meaning of the text. Some lines, however, are correct.
- If a line is correct, write **CORRECT** on your Answer Sheet.
- If there is an extra word in the line, write **the extra word** in CAPITAL LETTERS on your Answer Sheet.
- The exercise begins with two examples, (**0**) and (**00**).

Examples:	**0**	C	O	R	R	E	C	T	
	00	M	E						

Personal Assistant of the Year

0 Anne-Marie Garrard was shocked when it was announced that she had won the

00 Personal Assistant of the Year award. 'The other candidates seemed me

34 to be very strong, and I have to say I found that the selection procedure really

35 hard,' she says. 'I didn't think I had any chance of winning. When I heard my

36 name, my legs were so weak I could only hardly stand up,' she laughs. So

37 how is 'the best' personal assistant chosen from a group of so extremely good

38 and very different individuals? The final decision was reached after a

39 day-long session of the tests, interviews and exercises. Garrard believes

40 the skills she uses in her job helped her how to perform well. For instance, although

41 most of her work is for her company's Managing Director, she works for six bosses

42 in all, so she always tries out to be prepared for anything that might happen.

43 As for the future, her firm has closed for its summer break now; as soon as

44 they will open again, there is a pay rise waiting for her. But Garrard is not

45 going to be relax. She says, 'There's always room for personal development.
You must keep trying to improve.'

WRITING   45 minutes

PART ONE

- You are the Managing Director of a company whose profits have recently increased and you would like to reward staff for this.
- Write a **memo** to all staff:
  - thanking them for their contribution
  - explaining why profits increased
  - telling them what their reward will be.
- Write **40–50** words.

MEMO

To: **All Staff**

From:

Date: **7 December 2002**

Subject: **Staff Reward**

PART TWO

- Your company requires a taxi firm that it could use on a regular basis for staff and clients. Your secretary has selected two advertisements from the local newspaper.
- Look at the advertisements below, on which you have already made some handwritten notes.
- Then, using **all** your notes, write a **proposal** for your line manager, saying which firm you think your company should use.
- Write **120–140** words on a separate sheet.

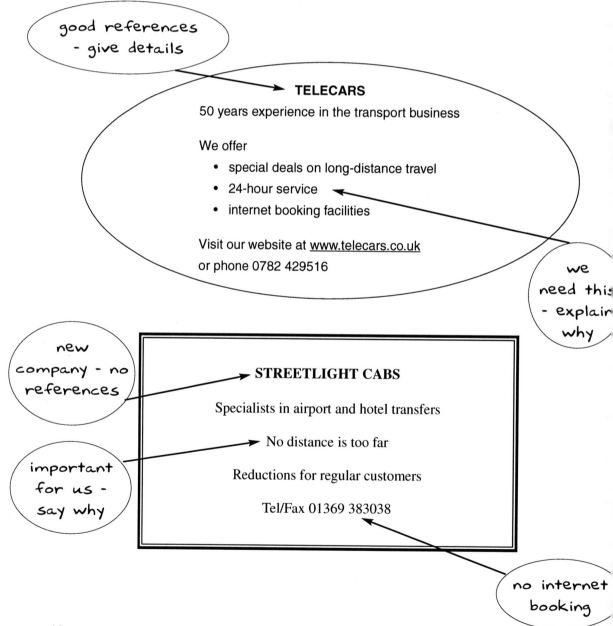

good references
- give details

TELECARS

50 years experience in the transport business

We offer
- special deals on long-distance travel
- 24-hour service
- internet booking facilities

Visit our website at www.telecars.co.uk
or phone 0782 429516

we
need this
- explain
why

new
company - no
references

STREETLIGHT CABS

Specialists in airport and hotel transfers

No distance is too far

Reductions for regular customers

Tel/Fax 01369 383038

important
for us -
say why

no internet
booking

LISTENING   40 minutes (including 10 minutes' transfer time)

PART ONE

Questions 1–12

- You will hear three telephone conversations or messages.
- Write **one** or **two** words or a number in the numbered spaces on the notes or forms below.
- After you have listened once, replay each recording.

Conversation One

(Questions 1–4)

- Look at the form below.
- You will hear a woman calling about training courses.

Oakleaf Business Training
CHANGES IN BOOKINGS

Caller's name: Enid Stevens

Course to be changed: (1) ....

Date change:

       old date: 8 July

       new date: (2) ....

Any further action:

send (3) ....for last January's course on

(4) ....

Conversation Two

(Questions 5–8)

- Look at the note below.
- You will hear a woman ringing about problems with a new telephone system.

WHILE YOU WERE OUT

Message for: Tony

From: Sheila Dallas of (5) ....

Taken by: Jeremy

Message

Re: the phone system we set up for them yesterday

- system doesn't include enough (6) ....

- they're unable to (7) .... internally

- invoice doesn't include discount on (8) ....

Please ring her back ASAP.

Conversation Three

(Questions 9–12)

- Look at the note below.
- You will hear a woman calling about the arrangements for a meeting.

TELEPHONE MESSAGE

For: John Fitzgerald

Name of caller: Elizabeth Parnell

Date: 7/12/2002

Time: 10.05

Message: Elizabeth will be in the USA until next Tuesday, for a (9) ....

Could you:

- change the meeting to (10) .... on Wednesday

- add an item to the agenda: the (11) .... ?

Please phone Elizabeth today at (12) ....

---

30   What is Simpson's planning to do?

    A   expand by taking over other companies
    B   reorganise the companies in the group
    C   increase its market share

You now have 10 minutes to transfer your answers to your Answer Sheet.

SPEAKING   14 minutes

PART ONE

The interview – about 3 minutes

In this part the interlocutor asks questions to each of the candidates in turn. You have to give information about yourself and express personal opinions.

PART TWO

'Mini presentation' – about 6 minutes

In this part of the test you are asked to give a short talk on a business topic. You have to choose one of the topics from the three below and then talk for about one minute. You have one minute to prepare your ideas.

A   WHAT IS IMPORTANT WHEN ...?
Selecting staff for promotion
● Attitude to work
● Current performance
●
●

B   WHAT IS IMPORTANT WHEN ...?
Considering a career change
● Further study or training
● Opportunities for future promotion
●
●

C   WHAT IS IMPORTANT WHEN ...?
Planning an advertising campaign
● Market research
● Selecting appropriate media
●
●

PART THREE

Discussion – about 5 minutes

In this part of the test you are given a discussion topic. You have 30 seconds to look at the prompt card, an example of which is below, and then about three minutes to discuss the topic with your partner. After that the examiner will ask you more questions related to the topic.

For **two** candidates

English Language Training

Your company is planning to offer 30 hours of English language training to employees.

You have been asked to help with the planning and organisation of the training.

Discuss the situation together, and decide:

- how to encourage employees to take part in the training
- what kind of schedule would be suitable for the training.

For **three** candidates

English Language Training

Your company is planning to offer 30 hours of English language training to employees.

You have been asked to help with the planning and organisation of the training.

Discuss the situation together, and decide:

- which staff would benefit most from English language training
- how to encourage employees to take part in the training
- what kind of schedule would be suitable for the training.

Follow-on questions

- What practical preparations would be necessary before running a foreign language course for employees? (Why?)

- What are the advantages of learning a foreign language with work colleagues?

- Are there any other foreign languages you would like to learn? (Why/Why not?)

- What ways of learning English are most helpful for people working in business? (Why?)

- What kind of help with language would you give to a foreign colleague who has just arrived to start a job in your company? (Why?)

- Do you think foreign language skills will continue to be useful for business in the future? (Why/Why not?)

Test 3

READING   1 hour

PART ONE

Questions 1–7

- Look at the statements below and the advice about how to deal with your boss on the opposite page.
- Which section (**A, B, C** or **D**) does each statement (**1–7**) refer to?
- For each statement (**1–7**), mark one letter (**A, B, C** or **D**) on your Answer Sheet.
- You will need to use some of these letters more than once.

Example:

0   Take notice of your boss's life away from work.

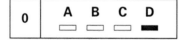

---

1   Listen to what your boss tells you about how well you are working.

2   Realise that your boss will occasionally need to be left alone.

3   Comment on your boss's work in a positive spirit.

4   Try to impress your boss with your thoroughness.

5   Do not hesitate to involve your boss if you have difficulties with your work.

6   Show your boss that you are capable of working at a higher level.

7   Speak to your boss, even about matters not directly related to your work.

MANAGE YOUR BOSS

Advice from four top business people on how you should treat your boss

A

The Consultant

No boss likes nasty surprises. Thinking you can solve a serious problem before he or she finds out is a doomed strategy. Much better to inform your boss about the situation early on, together with your suggested solution. Also, remember that bosses like praise as much as any employee. Do this without making it obvious, if only to earn the right to criticise (constructively, of course). 'Consideration' is the key word. Treat bosses as you hope to be treated – it should help you to move up to the next level.

B

The Director

Of course there are all the formal things in managing your boss – ensuring that you come to meetings well prepared, that you have a good eye for detail, and so on. But you also need to distinguish effectively between things that are important and things that are merely small details. Bosses like it if you can see 'the big picture' because they want to be able to delegate. So it's all about psychology, as well as performance.

C

The Chairman

Bosses want people to understand their objectives, their way of working and the pressures they are under. If you can understand what sort of individual your boss is, it is easier to appreciate why certain reactions might arise, and thus avoid problems. Also, keep the lines of communication with your boss open. You need to receive ongoing feedback on whether your work is effective, asking about what you do not understand, and, if necessary, discussing personal issues from outside the workplace. When the gap between you is reduced, so are the difficulties.

D

The Chief Executive

Understand that a boss will want to take the glory when things go well. After all, they take ultimate responsibility, so they deserve some of the credit. Also, find out about your boss's outside interests, as this can help to improve the relationship. You may find you have an interest in common. Similarly, recognise that everyone is human, and there are times when a request from you may be unwelcome. Get to know your boss's Personal Assistant, who can advise you when it is a good time to talk to him or her.

PART FOUR

Questions 19–33

- Read the extract below about a bank's human resources policy.
- Choose the best word or phrase to fill each gap from **A, B, C** or **D** on the opposite page.
- For each question (**19–33**), mark one letter (**A, B, C** or **D**) on your Answer Sheet.
- There is an example at the beginning, (**0**).

Human Resources Policy

CBA Bank was the largest financial institution to sign the employers' 'People Come First' code of practice in the early 1990s. In doing so, it committed itself to the highest (**0**) ...B... in human resources practices such as the communication of company (**19**) .... to employees, the setting of individual training and personal (**20**) .... plans, and the holding of regular performance (**21**) .... for all staff.

Like other organisations, CBA is replacing the traditional hierarchy with a flatter organisational structure which gives employees more broadly defined (**22**) .... within the company. The change is offering employees greater opportunities for work in cross-disciplinary project teams. As a result, interpersonal (**23**) .... are extremely important.

The policy seems to be working. There is a great deal of goodwill among employees, who (**24**) .... the fact that customer satisfaction is the organisation's chief aim. CBA claims to pursue this aim for its own (**25**) .... , rather than as a means of earning profits for shareholders.

An ability to relate to all kinds of people is the most important attribute CBA looks for in (**26**) .... recruits. Graduates are (**27**) .... for a two-year period and exposed to all (**28**) .... of retail financial services. By the end of this training period, they will have taken their Institute of Banking examination and, if they have (**29**) .... their performance targets, they will have (**30**) .... a job at the bank.

'On the whole, we are not looking for people straight out of college,' says human resources manager Mary Kemp. 'We would prefer that they had (**31**) .... some experience of life and had taken a year out between school and college to travel or do some kind of work.'

The company has recently introduced a new policy on pay, and it is now (**32**) .... to performance through bonus schemes, with the objective being to (**33**) .... employees for their achievements and effort.

Example:

  A levels   **B** standards   **C** guides   **D** measures

0	A B C D

19	**A** designs	**B** purposes	**C** ends	**D** objectives
20	**A** continuation	**B** extension	**C** development	**D** advancement
21	**A** reviews	**B** trials	**C** revisions	**D** judgements
22	**A** capacities	**B** parts	**C** roles	**D** elements
23	**A** abilities	**B** talents	**C** assets	**D** skills
24	**A** recommend	**B** honour	**C** respect	**D** obey
25	**A** sake	**B** reason	**C** behalf	**D** cause
26	**A** expected	**B** intended	**C** potential	**D** eventual
27	**A** taken on	**B** written in	**C** put on	**D** drawn in
28	**A** fields	**B** areas	**C** regions	**D** parts
29	**A** arrived	**B** done	**C** passed	**D** met
30	**A** secured	**B** reached	**C** confirmed	**D** fixed
31	**A** gained	**B** won	**C** earned	**D** realised
32	**A** attached	**B** linked	**C** combined	**D** joined
33	**A** return	**B** reward	**C** recompense	**D** refund

PART FIVE

Questions 34–45

- Read the text below about meetings.
- In most of the lines (**34–45**) there is one extra word. It is either grammatically incorrect or does not fit in with the meaning of the text. Some lines, however, are correct.
- If a line is correct, write **CORRECT** on your Answer Sheet.
- If there is an extra word in the line, write **the extra word** in CAPITAL LETTERS on your Answer Sheet.
- The exercise begins with two examples, (**0**) and (**00**).

Examples:

0	I	T						
00	C	O	R	R	E	C	T	

Meetings That Work

0	A vital skill for anyone running a business it is the ability to communicate
00	effectively. This is particularly important in a meeting where complex arguments
34	need to be put forward and where it is too vital to get the best out of the situation
35	and those present in as little time as possible. Before calling a meeting, ask
36	yourself if you actually need one, since so many are unproductive results and do
37	not really need to take place. Sending an email or by using another means of
38	communication, such as a simple phone call, might achieve the desired results in
39	half the time. Having established the need for a meeting, so inform those you
40	wish to attend and ask people to be punctual. Concerning the key to a good
41	meeting is an agenda, which needs to be sent out in advance and should state the
42	date, time and location. It should also contain the names of those ones who will
43	be present and set that out, starting with the most important, the points for
44	discussion. Ask in advance for suggestions for items to be discussed about but
45	set a deadline for submissions in order to reduce the amount of time that has to be
	spent under 'Any Other Business'.

WRITING   45 minutes

WRITING

PART ONE

- You are the Managing Director of a manufacturing company. Your factory will soon have a visit from health and safety inspectors.
- Write an **email** to your department heads:
  - saying how long the inspection will take
  - explaining why the inspection is necessary
  - telling them how they should prepare for the inspection.
- Write **40–50** words.

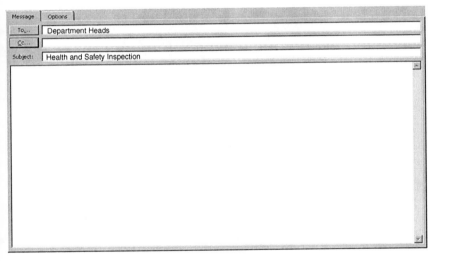

PART TWO

- You work for Norlec, an electrical goods manufacturer, and your company director wants to find out which methods of advertising are the most effective. Recently the marketing department has asked customers how they first learnt about Norlec.
- Look at the information below, on which you have already made some handwritten notes.
- Then, using **all** your handwritten notes, write your **report**.
- Write **120–140** words.

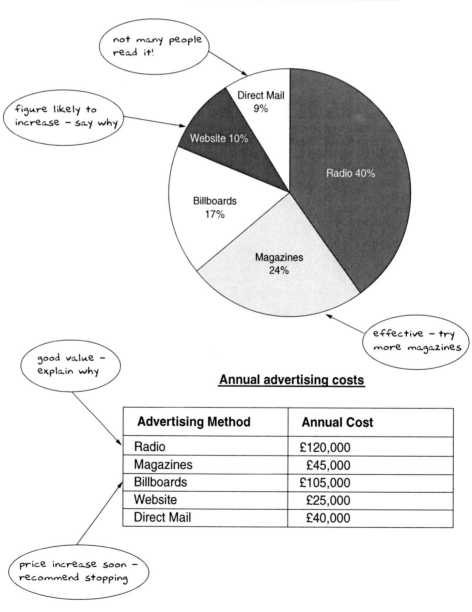

How customers learnt about Norlec

not many people read it!

figure likely to increase – say why

Direct Mail 9%

Website 10%

Radio 40%

Billboards 17%

Magazines 24%

effective – try more magazines

good value – explain why

Annual advertising costs

Advertising Method	Annual Cost
Radio	£120,000
Magazines	£45,000
Billboards	£105,000
Website	£25,000
Direct Mail	£40,000

price increase soon – recommend stopping

LISTENING   40 minutes (including 10 minutes' transfer time)

PART ONE

Questions 1–12

- You will hear three telephone conversations or messages.
- Write **one** or **two** words or a number in the numbered spaces on the notes or forms below.
- After you have listened once, replay each recording.

Conversation One

(Questions 1–4)

- Look at the form below.
- You will hear a conversation between two salespeople at BAS, a software company.

RECORD OF SALES CALL

Salesperson: Alan Barnard

Client: Electrolin

Products client is interested in: **(1)** ....

Name of contact: Steve McCormack

Contact's position: **(2)** ....

New contact ✓   Existing contact ☐

Action required: Arrange a **(3)** ....

Location: At BAS (factory)

Level of priority: **(4)** ....

Name of salesperson to follow up enquiry: Janet Hughes

Conversation Two

(Questions 5–8)

● Look at the notes below.
● You will hear a sales representative phoning a colleague at Head Office.

TELEPHONE NOTES

Re: Sales Literature for Paris Show

30 more copies of the (5) ....
catalogue needed.

Correct the wheel (6) ....
for children's cycles on page 3 of leaflet.

Query re missing (7) ....
for lightweight touring cycles.

Send order forms for (8) ....

Conversation Three

(Questions 9–12)

- Look at the form below.
- You will hear a customer telephoning a company about a delivery.

DELIVERY NOTE

Customer: Planet Design Shops

Order No: 300571

Address for delivery: (9) ....

Instructions for driver:

Parking available in (10) ....

Give (11) .... to customer.

Collect old (12) .... from customer.

---

29 The final company visited by the speaker

    A   has rapidly gained a world-wide reputation.

    B   has recently increased its production area.

    C   has received a loan to improve technology.

30 The speaker recommends the final company because

    A   it has agreed to reduce its prices for large orders.

    B   it can produce goods within the required timescale.

    C   its products passed the inspection test she carried out.

You now have 10 minutes to transfer your answers to your Answer Sheet.

SPEAKING   14 minutes

PART ONE

The interview – about 3 minutes

In this part the interlocutor asks questions to each of the candidates in turn. You have to give information about yourself and express personal opinions.

PART TWO

'Mini presentation' – about 6 minutes

In this part of the test you are asked to give a short talk on a business topic. You have to choose one of the topics from the three below and then talk for about one minute. You have one minute to prepare your ideas.

A   WHAT IS IMPORTANT WHEN ...?

Choosing transport for a business trip
- Convenience
- Cost-effectiveness
-
-

B   WHAT IS IMPORTANT WHEN ...?

Aiming for promotion
- Quality of performance
- Company loyalty
-
-

C   WHAT IS IMPORTANT WHEN ...?

Exporting goods or services for the first time
- Personal contacts
- Professional advice
-
-

PART THREE

Discussion – about 5 minutes

In this part of the test you are given a discussion topic. You have 30 seconds to look at the prompt card, an example of which is below, and then about three minutes to discuss the topic with your partner. After that the examiner will ask you more questions related to the topic.

For **two** candidates

Teamwork

Your company is sending a small group of employees away together for three days to encourage them to work as a team.

You have been asked to help plan the programme.

Discuss the situation together, and decide:

- what practical arrangements the company needs to make before the trip
- which work and leisure activities would be suitable for the group.

For **three** candidates

Teamwork

Your company is sending a small group of employees away together for three days to encourage them to work as a team.

You have been asked to help plan the programme.

Discuss the situation together, and decide:

- what practical arrangements the company needs to make before the trip
- which work and leisure activities would be suitable for the group
- how to evaluate the success of the trip.

Follow-on questions

- What preparations might the participants need to make before going away? (Why?)

- What might be the disadvantages of working as part of a team? (Why?)

- Would you like to take part in a programme for developing teamwork? (Why/Why not?)

- What kinds of activities would you like to participate in with colleagues outside work? (Why?)

- How might a company measure the success of a training programme?

- Do you think staff training is always of benefit to a company? (Why/Why not?)

PART TWO

Questions 8–12

- Read the article below giving advice to managers about performance reviews.
- Choose the best sentence from the opposite page to fill each of the gaps.
- For each gap (**8–12**), mark one letter (**A–G**) on your Answer Sheet.
- Do not use any letter more than once.
- There is an example at the beginning, (**0**).

STAFF APPRAISALS

A director of the advertising agency owned by tycoon Bob Jacoby once grumbled that he wasn't enjoying his work. Jacoby's reply was, 'I don't pay you good money to enjoy yourself. If you enjoy working here, you should be paying me money.' Jacoby's sentiments used to be common. (**0**) ....*G*... . Happily, things have changed. Most organisations now undertake regular staff appraisals, at which employees have the opportunity to discuss one-to-one with their line manager their ambitions and hopes, their strengths and weaknesses, their achievements and their disasters. But it is worth remembering how new all this is, and why.

For a start, appraising isn't something many managers do naturally, of their own accord. They often find appraisals difficult to handle and have to be made to carry them out. Appraisal systems have become widespread partly as a result of employment legislation, but more particularly because companies have learned that such assessments can work to their advantage. (**8**) .... The company can improve its collective performance by helping employees to improve their individual performance.

Managers who use appraisals need to approach them very carefully. They should bear in mind their own experiences of being appraised when in junior positions, recalling which appraisals were helpful, which were not, and why. In most cases, their own bosses did their homework, checking out the job specification, the C.V. and

any previous reports. (**9**) .... As a result, a lot of time would have been wasted, debating exactly what had happened and when.

Being prepared and appreciating what it is like to be on the receiving end are, indeed, the keys to successful appraising. It is important to begin an appraisal by giving members of staff a chance to express their own views about their performance. (**10**) .... Any information gained from colleagues is normally given in a positive spirit, since nowadays everyone understands appraisals and appreciates that they are carried out with good intentions.

The atmosphere in the appraisal should be one of positive and open discussion about how the employee is performing in the company. (**11**) .... Some individuals will feel unjustly criticised when their boss makes comments on their performance. Others will respond fiercely to a critical assessment – although if they defend themselves passionately, that is no bad thing!

Finally, it is important to regard appraisals as part of a continuing process. (**12**) .... Instead, they should be followed up with friendly questions from time to time, making it clear to employees that new goals and strategies suggested in them are to be taken seriously and are to be acted upon.

If these pieces of advice are followed, it is hoped that both the employees and the company as a whole will benefit from the experience.

Example:

0	A	B	C	D	E	F	G
	☐	☐	☐	☐	☐	☐	▬

A However, managers must take great care in this respect.

B Only after that should managers put forward their own points, which are likely to include comments collected from others in the organisation.

C They should not be forgotten as soon as they are over.

D Like many other aspects of free enterprise, appraisals are an excellent example of underlying self-interest.

E Sometimes the appraiser goes too far the other way and fails to communicate problem areas and scope for improvement.

F If they relied on memory, they probably got things wrong.

G Employees were paid, and they obeyed; if they didn't like it, they could leave.

PART THREE

Questions 13–18

- Read the article below about bringing new products onto the market and the questions on the opposite page.
- For each question (**13–18**), mark one letter (**A, B, C** or **D**) on your Answer Sheet.

Market Entry – The Pioneer

Marc Crystal discusses the 'be first to market' principle

The timing of market entry is critical to the success of a new product. A company has two alternatives: it can compete to enter a new product market first – otherwise known as 'pioneering' – or it can wait for a competitor to take the lead, and then follow once the market has been established. Despite the limitations of existing research, nobody denies that there are advantages to being a pioneering company. Over the years, there has been a good deal of evidence to show a performance advantage for pioneers.

For many new products, customers are initially unsure about the contribution of product characteristics and features to the product's value. Preferences for different characteristics and their desired levels are learned over time. This enables the pioneering company to shape customer preferences in its favour. It sets the standard to which customers refer in evaluating followers' products. The pioneering product can become the classic or 'original' product for the whole category, opening up a flood of similar products onto the market, as exemplified by *Walkman* and *Polaroid*.

The pioneering product is a bigger novelty when it appears on the market, and is therefore more likely than those that follow to capture customer and distributor attention. In addition, a pioneer's advertising is not mixed up with competitors' campaigns. Even in the long term, followers must continue to spend more on advertising to achieve the same effect as pioneers. The pioneers can set standards for distribution, occupy the best locations or select the best distributors, which can give them easier access to customers. For example, in many US cities the coffee chain *Starbucks*, as the first to market, was able to open coffee bars in better known locations than its competitors. In many industrial markets, distributors are not keen to take on second and third products, particularly when the product is technically complex or requires large inventories of spare parts.

'Switching costs' arise when investments are required in order to switch to another product. For example, many people have developed skills in using the traditional 'qwerty' keyboard. Changing to the presumably more efficient 'dvorak' keyboard would require relearning how to type, an investment that in many cases would exceed the expected benefits in efficiency. Switching costs also arise when the quality of a product is difficult to assess. People who live abroad often experience a similar 'cost' when simple purchase decisions such as buying detergent, toothpaste or coffee suddenly become harder because the trusted brand from home is no longer available. Pioneering products have the first chance to become this trusted brand. Consequently, the companies that follow must work hard to convince customers to bear the costs and risks of switching to an untried brand of unknown quality.

Unlike other consumer sectors, the value to customers of many high technology products relies not only on their features but also on the total number of users. For example, the value of a videophone depends on the number of people using the same or a compatible system. A pioneer obviously has the opportunity to build a large user base before competitors enter the market. This reduces followers' ability to introduce differentiated products. There are other advantages of a large user base, such as the ability to share computer files with other users. Thus, software companies are often willing to give away products to build the market quickly and set a standard.

13 In the first paragraph, the writer points out that

 A there is general agreement on the benefits of pioneering products.
 B companies are still uncertain about how to market new products.
 C most companies prefer to market new products independently.
 D there are now guidelines to help those who wish to pioneer.

14 According to the information in the second paragraph, how do customers approach new products?

 A They take some time to develop a liking for them.
 B They make comparisons with other new products.
 C They need some persuasion to purchase them.
 D They consider cost an important feature.

15 The writer refers to *Walkman* and *Polaroid* because they were

 A better than any of their followers.
 B copied many times by their followers.
 C quickly accepted by consumers.
 D designed for a particular market.

16 When pioneering products are promoted, the writer notes that

 A a heavy financial investment is required.
 B a wide variety of advertising methods must be used.
 C a clear message is likely to be communicated.
 D a long campaign is usually necessary.

17 In the keyboard example, the 'costs' the writer is referring to are concerned with

 A the price of the products.
 B the quality of the products.
 C the need for user training.
 D the lack of useful information.

18 According to the final paragraph, the high technology market differs from other consumer markets in that

 A it is still a relatively new area of consumerism.
 B it is not dependent on product characteristics alone.
 C there are so many different types of product on the market.
 D there is such a great demand for high technology products.

PART TWO

- You are in charge of technical resources in your company. You have just received a letter from the Customer Services Manager at JLM Communications, who are installing a new telephone switchboard at your offices.
- Look at part of the letter below, on which you have already made some handwritten notes.
- Then, using **all** your handwritten notes, write a **letter** to JLM's Customer Services Manager.
- Write **120–140** words.
- You do not need to provide postal addresses.

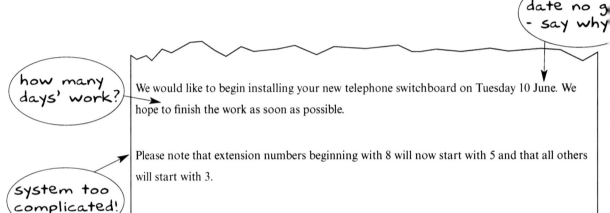

date no g
- say why

how many days' work?

We would like to begin installing your new telephone switchboard on Tuesday 10 June. We hope to finish the work as soon as possible.

Please note that extension numbers beginning with 8 will now start with 5 and that all others will start with 3.

system too complicated!

If you have any technical queries, please contact our technical representative at our main office.

name?

A copy of our invoice is attached.

will pay when job finished - say why

LISTENING 40 minutes (including 10 minutes' transfer time)

PART ONE

Questions 1–12

- You will hear three telephone conversations or messages.
- Write **one** or **two** words or a number in the numbered spaces on the notes or forms below.
- After you have listened once, replay each recording.

Conversation One

(Questions 1–4)

- Look at the form below.
- You will hear a woman leaving an answerphone message for a company.

Telephone Message for Max Jacobs

Message from Alison Gates of Merland Healthcare:

Would like us to develop a (1) .... for them.

Recommended by a (2) ....

Alison Gates's email address: agates@
(3) .... .com

Please arrange to meet her and the
(4) .... at Merland's.

Conversation Two

(Questions 5–8)

- Look at the notes below.
- You will hear a marketing manager reporting on sales of a product.

MusicMate Cassette Player

Success of the product is due to low cost
& (5) ....

Sales are currently highest in

(6) ....

We need new (7) ...., but too
expensive

Recommended strategy: increase

(8) ....

Conversation Three

(Questions 9–12)

Look at the notes below.
• You will hear a woman phoning for information about a meeting.

NOTES

Shareholders' Meeting

Location: (9) ....

Requirements

• Seating for: (10) ....

• Equipment: five (11) ....
        two OHPS

• Photocopied materials: agenda
        (12) ....

PART THREE

Discussion – about 5 minutes

In this part of the test you are given a discussion topic. You have 30 seconds to look at the prompt card, an example of which is below, and then about three minutes to discuss the topic with your partner. After that the examiner will ask you more questions related to the topic.

For **two** candidates

> **Entertaining Foreign Clients**
>
> Your company is entertaining a group of foreign clients for three days, including one non-working day.
>
> You have been asked to plan a programme for the visit.
>
> Discuss the situation together, and decide:
>
> - what kinds of activities would be suitable for the visit
>
> - what information it would be useful to know about the clients before finalising the programme.

For **three** candidates

> **Entertaining Foreign Clients**
>
> Your company is entertaining a group of foreign clients for three days, including one non-working day.
>
> You have been asked to plan a programme for the visit.
>
> Discuss the situation together, and decide:
>
> - what kinds of activities would be suitable for the visit
>
> - which members of staff should accompany the visitors
>
> - what information it would be useful to know about the clients before finalising the programme.

Follow-on questions

- What kinds of arrangements need to be made before foreign visitors arrive? (Why?)

- Are there any disadvantages for a company in having a visit from foreign clients? (Why/Why not?)

- Where would you take foreign visitors in your home town? (Why?)

- Would you enjoy looking after business visitors for a few days? (Why/Why not?)

- What problems might there be when socialising with foreign business people? (Why?)

- What are the long-term benefits of establishing personal contacts with foreign clients? (Why?)

KEY

Test 1 Reading

Part 1

1 C   2 A   3 B   4 D   5 A   6 B
7 C

Part 2

8 D   9 C   10 E   11 B   12 F

Part 3

13 D   14 A   15 C   16 B   17 B
18 C

Part 4

19 B	20 A	21 D	22 A	23 C
24 C	25 D	26 A	27 B	28 C
29 D	30 B	31 C	32 B	33 B

Part 5

34 ITSELF	35 IN	36 CORRECT
37 WHILE	38 SEEN	39 FROM
40 CORRECT	41 THOSE	42 FOR
43 WITH	44 THAT	45 CORRECT

Test 1 Writing

Part 1

Sample A

> To: P. Jones
> From: Luisa Gambon
> Date: 21 November 2002
> Subject: Lateness
>
> Mr Jones,
>
> I have noticed that you often arrive late for work, especially on Monday mornings. As your colleagues are starting to complain about that, you understand that unless this habit changes, I will take disciplinary action against you.
> Come and see me tomorrow at 9 a.m. in my office.
> Thank you

Band 5

All content points are covered, using natural sounding language and a consistently appropriate tone.

Sample B

> To: P. Jones
> From: Manager
> Date: 21 November 2002
> Subject: Lateness
>
> Hi, Jones
>
> Nowadays you arrives late for work very often. I feel you may have particular reasons for it. But if you keep going your lateness, other staff in the office may be late like you. I'm worrying about it. How about considering of being more punctual?
>
> Thanks!

Band 3

All the content points are covered, though at times the register is not always entirely successful. There is evidence of an adequate range of structures and vocabulary for this level, but with some non-impeding errors.

Part 2

Sample C

> Report on customer complaints
>
> INTRODUCTION
> This report has the purpose of presenting the reasons for customer complaints in 2002.
>
> FIELDINGS
> The customer complaints received in 2002 were 300 in January. Then they increased to 540 in February because of the computer system's breakdown.
> In March they fell to 230 because an improved order system was introduced.
> The reasons for complaints from January to March were analysed:
> • firstly the company received complaints for incorrect orders delivered. These errors were fewer in March.
> • secondly the time taken to deliver is too high, but the company has planned to recruit new agents.
> • Finally customers complain for the poor product quality. In order to solve this problem more quality controls are making.
>
> CONCLUSIONS
> At the moment all customers aren't satisfied but many measures have been taken to improve their satisfaction.

Band 4

There is a satisfactory range of structures, with some errors, but these do not impede understanding. The content points are adequately covered, and the register is appropriate. The information is generally well organised, using headings and other discourse markers.

Sample D

Customer Complaints Reports
(2002 Jan–Mar)

Background
- Number of customers complains received showed very high points in February
- It became less half than February's in March.

Analysis
- The breakdown of computer system in February lead to a lot of complaints.
- On the other hand the introduction of improved order system decrease the amount.
- Fewer incorrect order delivered in March. It result in few complaints.
- More than half of complaints are because of late deliver.
- Unsatisfactory product quality's complaints showed 28% of all.

Recommendation
- To improve delivery system is important, it leads the decrease of complaints. It should be improved.
- To reduce poor quality product. Products should be cheack before shipping.

Band 2

The organisation of the report is reasonable, as is the register and format. However, not all content points are adequately addressed, a limited range of language is used, and there are some distracting errors.

Test 1   Listening

Part 1

1 JAYE
2 CUSTOMER SERVICES
3 OFFICE ASSISTANT
4 457.60
5 EUROPE HOLIDAYS
6 BUSINESS CARDS
7 MARKETING EXECUTIVES
8 (THE) (COMPANY) LOGO
9 INFORMATION PACK
10 PARK HOTEL
11 FRONT GATE
12 NEW DESIGNS

Part 2

13 E	14 B	15 G	16 F	17 A
18 C	19 G	20 H	21 E	22 B

Part 3

23 B	24 B	25 C	26 A	27 C
28 B	29 A	30 C		

Tapescript

Listening Test 1

This is the Business English Certificate Vantage 2, Listening Test 1.

Part One. Questions 1 to 12.

You will hear three telephone conversations or messages.

Write one or two words or a number in the numbered spaces on the notes or forms below.

After you have listened once, replay each recording.

Conversation One. Questions 1 to 4.

Look at the form below.

You will hear a man asking a colleague for information about a former employee.

You have 15 seconds to read through the form.

[pause]

Now listen, and fill in the spaces.

Woman: Personnel . . .
Man: Hello, it's Tim here, from Finance.
Woman: Hi, Tim.
Man: I've had a letter from the tax office about a student who worked here last summer – I wonder if you could look him up in your records.
Woman: Sure, what's the name?
Man: The surname's Jaye. First name Stephen.
Woman: How does he spell his surname?
Man: J-A-Y-E. Got that?
Woman: Oh yes, here we are . . . lives at a hundred and eighty-three School Road, Barnfield . . .
Man: Yes, that's the one.
Woman: And you say he was working in Finance?

Man: Uhm, Customer Services, actually.

Woman: Aah – they had lots of students working for them last summer.

Man: Well, the tax people want to know his exact job title – I'm not sure why.

Woman: Mm, let me see . . . He was an office assistant.

Man: Right, got that. They also want to know about his monthly earnings.

Woman: Let's have a look . . . five hundred and thirty-eight pounds seventy a month . . . Oh, sorry, he was a scale one, so that's four hundred and fifty-seven pounds sixty. Anything else?

Man: That's fine, thanks. I'll send them the information today . . .

[pause]

Now listen to the recording again.

[pause]

Conversation Two. Questions 5 to 8.

Look at the note below.

You will hear a man describing a problem with an order.

You have 15 seconds to read through the note.

[pause]

Now listen, and fill in the spaces.

Woman: Hello, Blackwell Printers. Julie Davidson speaking. How may I help you?

Man: Hello. This is Mark Jones from Europe Holidays. I was hoping to speak to Steven Kirby about the stationery you're printing for us.

Woman: I'm afraid Steven's away until Friday.

Man: Oh – you see I'm not very happy with the business cards and I wanted to see if I could make a couple of changes to the paper too.

Woman: Would you like me to pass on a message?

Man: Yes, please. The thing is, I've just received your proofs – the cards themselves are fine, but you seem to have misunderstood the quantities. I'm sure I asked for five hundred for each of the marketing executives and seven hundred and fifty for me but you've put everyone down for seven hundred and fifty.

Woman: Right, I've made a note of that. Is there anything else?

Man: Yes, well this is my mistake really. Could you ask Steven to move the company logo further to the left? It's too close to the address at the moment. I think that's all for now. Thanks.

[pause]

Now listen to the recording again.

[pause]

Conversation Three. Questions 9 to 12.

Look at the notes below.

You will hear a woman making the arrangements for a delegation who are going to visit her company.

You have 15 seconds to read through the notes.

[pause]

Now listen, and fill in the spaces.

Woman: Geoff?

Man: Yes?

Woman: I just want to finalise the preparations for the delegation next week.

Man: Certainly. It's Thursday, isn't it?

Woman: Yes. Now, can you make sure that each of them gets a name badge and an information pack. The badges are done, but you'll need to prepare the packs with all the relevant information.

Man: Ok, that shouldn't take too long. What about catering?

Woman: Coffee's organised for eleven and three, but lunch – it's at one – we need to reserve it for twelve people . . . The office restaurant is closed next week . . . can you ring the Park Hotel? The Grand Hotel was a bit disappointing last time.

Man: I'll get onto that.

Woman: Now, they'll be coming straight from the station, and their taxi will bring them to the front gate, so make sure you're there to greet them. That'll be about ten.

Man: Ten. And then . . .

Woman: Into Reception, I think. Make sure the new designs are on display, I want them to see those first.

Man: OK.

Woman: Let me know when it's all finalised. Bye.

[pause]

Now listen to the recording again.

[pause]

That is the end of Part One. You now have 20 seconds to check your answers.

[pause]

Part Two. Questions 13 to 22.

Section One. Questions 13 to 17.

You will hear five short recordings.

For each recording, decide which type of document the speaker is talking about.

Write one letter (A–H) next to the number of the recording.

Do not use any letter more than once.

After you have listened once, replay the recordings.

You have 15 seconds to read the list A–H.

[pause]

Now listen, and decide which type of document each speaker is talking about.

[pause]

Thirteen

Woman: Well no wonder the bank's returned it unpaid. Look, the figures don't match the amount in words. I expect someone was filling it in in too much of a hurry. Let's see, we'd better issue another one straight away to pay Mrs Burton, because it'll be another three weeks if we wait for the next cycle of payments. Her expenses on that sales trip were pretty high, and it wouldn't be fair to keep her waiting much longer.

[pause]

Fourteen

Man: Some of the suppliers are already asking about the increases. I'll check, but I seem to remember from last week's meeting that in the end we agreed on three per cent. So what I'll do is go down each column and calculate the new amounts, and then it can be printed in time to be inserted into the new brochures. Can you check the figures for me, though, before it goes to the printers?

[pause]

Fifteen

Woman: We've just received the paperwork from you about cleaning our premises, and I have to say that it doesn't reflect what we agreed in our conversation last week. For one thing, it says that we have to supply our security code, and for another it specifies monthly payment in advance, and I told you both of those were out of the question. I'm afraid I really can't sign this. Could you send me a revised one?

[pause]

Sixteen

Man: Of course, this only gives a very general picture. But as you can see, cash is a particularly healthy area. That's even when we take into account regular outgoings on loans and leasing equipment, which are included in the final totals. And even more significantly, unpaid orders are actually excluded from the final calculation. These represent a sum of approximately thirty thousand pounds. With that in mind, we can say that the company's overall position is still strong.

[pause]

Seventeen

Woman: I've just asked the Arden Conference Centre about availability for our next training seminar, and they said they still haven't been paid for the one before last, which should have been dealt with six months ago. I've had to ask them to send a duplicate! We really must be careful. Arden give us very favourable prices, but we haven't got a contract with them – Can you deal with it straight away so we stay in their good books?

[pause]

Now listen to the recordings again.

[pause]

Section Two. Questions 18 to 22.

You will hear another five recordings.

For each recording, decide what the speaker's purpose is.

Write one letter (A–H) next to the number of the recording.

Do not use any letter more than once.

After you have listened once, replay the recordings.

You have 15 seconds to read the list A–H.

[pause]

Now listen, and decide what each speaker's purpose is.

[pause]

Eighteen

Man: Hello. This is Guy Cooper from Centron Electronics here. I believe you rang for some advice about your alarm system, which isn't functioning properly. The message I got said you weren't sure if you needed someone to come and sort it out, or if we could advise you over the phone. Well perhaps you'd like to get back to me as soon as it's convenient and tell me exactly what the problem is, and I'll see what I can do.

[pause]

Nineteen

Woman: Well, as you say, Redlon has been supplying us for years but, quite honestly, two-thirds of the complaints we receive about our products are actually due to faults in components we've had from Redlon. So I talked to the Production Manager and he agreed that I should look at some alternatives. FutureWorld's range is fine for us, and one of their customers who I spoke to recommended them highly, so that's why we've changed to using them.

[pause]

Twenty

Woman: The competition's getting tougher, and you know we're facing serious problems. We need to see more benefit from the undeniably hard work we're putting in, and this means saying no to jobs which aren't profitable. It would be much more beneficial to put all our efforts into winning higher-margin contracts. So the way I feel you can help most is by identifying the types of contacts which will bring in the income we need in order to ensure our future.

[pause]

Twenty-one

Man: John Woods here, phoning about the project we discussed earlier. Could you give me a ring so that we can talk about it a bit more? I've done a few calculations and I'm beginning to wonder whether it's really a practical proposition. I still think the project's got potential, but there are significant additional costs which we hadn't taken into account. So could you get back to me as soon as you can, please?

[pause]

Twenty-two

Woman: Hello, Sally here, from Pagwell Paints, returning your call. I'm very sorry you aren't happy with the latest consignment you've had from us. It's rather strange, because following your complaint about the last delivery, we did in fact take action to change the specifications in the way you suggested. So it isn't quite fair to

say that we ignored your advice. I know it's important to achieve the consistency that you require, but perhaps your recommendation wasn't exactly what's needed.

[pause]

Now listen to the recordings again.

[pause]

That is the end of Part Two.

[pause]

Part Three. Questions 23 to 30.

You will hear the chairman of a business institute making a speech about new business awards that his institute has sponsored.

For each question 23–30, mark one letter (A, B or C) for the correct answer.

After you have listened once, replay the recording.

You have 45 seconds to read through the questions.

[pause]

Now listen, and mark A, B or C.

[pause]

Man: Who are the managers of the best innovation developments in British industry? That was the question which the first Business Today Innovation Awards set out to answer.

This project is all about rewarding good practice and performance. So, rather than simply recognising excellence in the design of specific products, or analysing their financial impact on profits, the awards set out to take an objective look at exactly how companies manage the development process itself.

Over three hundred and fifty organisations entered the competition and were initially reduced to about forty. Then, after further careful checking, a short list of just fourteen of them was arrived at. These finalists, all manufacturers, were then visited by the competition judges, a panel of four chief executives from leading companies. The panel toured the finalists' facilities, received presentations on the companies and their projects, and interviewed the key development team members. The products varied enormously in their scale, function and degree of technology – from bread for a supermarket chain to a printer inside an automatic cash dispenser.

initially the organisers were concerned that this range could create difficulties in the assessment process. But this fear proved baseless, as most elements in the innovation process are shared by all manufacturers.

Interestingly, the finalists broke down into two distinct and equal groups: large firms with one thousand employees or more and small firms with two hundred and fifty employees or fewer. With both groups the judges decided to concentrate on two of the clearest indicators of a successful innovation process, which are: how well the new product is combined with the company's existing business, and secondly, how well the innovation methods are recorded and understood. Small firms naturally tend to do well in the first category since they have fewer layers of management and thus much shorter communication lines. But they seem to put less emphasis on creating formal development methods which would be repeatable in future innovations.

Large firms, on the other hand, have difficulty integrating the new development within their existing business for reasons of scale. But they tend to succeed in achieving well-documented and repeatable development methods. This is because larger companies, with their clear emphasis on training, fixed management structure and administrative systems, require more formal, daily record-keeping from their staff.

So what were the key questions the judges had in mind when assessing the finalists? One of the most important areas concerned how thoroughly a company checks what is happening in other fields in order to incorporate new ideas into the development process. Many of the finalists impressed in the area. Natura, for example, had demonstrated genuine energy in searching for new ways of producing their range of speciality breads. They had looked at styles of home cooking in different countries, as well as the possibility of exploiting new production technologies in order to achieve equally good results but on a high-volume production line.

What then occupied much of the judges' thoughts was the quality of the links which the development team established with senior management, suppliers, the market and manufacturing. The best examples of the first category were found in small firms, where the individual entrepreneur at the top was clearly driving the innovation forward.

Links with suppliers were also seen as an important factor, but not all supplier experiences were positive. Occasionally serious problems had to be solved where suppliers were working hard to meet specifications, but the companies that the suppliers were using to adapt their machinery were not so efficient. This led to disappointing faults or fluctuations in quality.

But in conclusion the awards demonstrate that innovation isn't just for high-tech internet companies. You can also be successful in mature markets with determination and skill.

[pause]

Now listen to the recording again.

[pause]

That is the end of Part Three. You now have ten minutes to transfer your answers to your Answer Sheet.

Note: Teacher, stop the recording here and time ten minutes. Remind students when there is **one** minute remaining.

[pause]

That is the end of the test.

Test 2   Reading

Part 1

1 B	2 C	3 A	4 D	5 D
6 B	7 C			

Part 2

8 C	9 B	10 E	11 A	12 D

Part 3

13 D	14 C	15 A	16 A	17 C
18 B				

Part 4

19 D	20 D	21 A	22 C	23 A
24 C	25 B	26 A	27 A	28 D
29 C	30 A	31 C	32 D	33 B

Part 5

34 THAT	35 CORRECT		36 ONLY
37 SO	38 CORRECT	39 THE	
40 HOW	41 CORRECT		42 OUT
43 CORRECT	44 WILL	45 BE	

Test 2 Writing

Part 1

Sample A

> To: All Staff
> From: Managing Director
> Date: 7 December
> Subject: Staff reward
>
> I would like to thank you for the contribution in increasing the company's profit. The profit increased due to very hard work and long working hours. Each of the staff will receive an envelope with a reward on Tuesday. The reward is a trip to Hawaii, and I hope that this will be the perfect reward. Enjoy!
>
> Thank you

Band 4
All points are adequately covered and developed. There is an adequate range of language, though with some repetition.

Sample B

> To: All Staff
> From: Paul Blake
> Date: 7 December 2002
> Subject: Staff reward
>
> I am very pleased to tell everybody that our company was make a great profit in this year. Thank a lot everybody's contribution for the company. Due to work hard, the management decided that every body would get the oppotunity to add the salary and paid holiday.

Band 2
All the content points are addressed, although poor control of basic structures, e.g. *'was make'*, *'oppotunity to add the salary'*, obscure the message at times.

Part 2

Sample C

> Introduction.
> The purpose of this report is to assess and recomend a taxi firm that will become our regular transporter. We will need them especially during next year trade fair and conferences. There are two firms to assess.
> Findings:
> As regards to Telecars we have a good references on them. It is very experienced traditional firm and is also very reliable. They provide 24-hours service that is useful during night meetings and negotiations. StreetlightCabs is brand new company and there are no references on them. But they provide long distance routes which we use very often and they are also cheaper. On the other hand they don't have web page and so internet booking isn't available.
> Conclusion:
> I recommend to choose Telecars because of their reliability, long tradition and well trained staff.

Band 4
All the content points are covered and are well organised. The range of language is good, and though some errors occur, these do not obscure the message. The register is appropriate.

Sample D

> From: The General Manager
> To: The line manager
>
> THE PROPOSAL
>
> In order to have a taxi firm that it could use on a regular bases for our staff and clients, we should choose the better one. The things following below are my proposal. In the advertisement of TELECARS, it gaves details. It's a good reference. The three details are useful for us. we need the 24-hour service, because our company is runned for whole day, and we need meet the clients at any time.
> Compared with the other one, I think the one of STREETLIGHTCABS is not well. It's a new company and it has not any references. The distance is important for us because we are in the urban. If no distance is too far, it not good for our business. And it also has no internet booking.
> So I think the advertisement of TELECARS fits for our requires.

Band 2
An attempt is made to address all the language points, but this is not always successful. Generally the range of language is fairly limited and basic errors occur.

Test 2   Listening

Part 1

1 TAKING MINUTES
2 13(TH) OCTOBER
3 CERTIFICATE
4 CUSTOMER SERVICE
5 WORLDNET/WORLD NET
6 OUTSIDE LINES
7 TRANSFER CALLS
8 (THE) EQUIPMENT
9 TRADE FAIR
10 AFTER LUNCH
11 REVISED BUDGETS
12 HEAD OFFICE

Part 2

13 H	14 E	15 F	16 A	17 D
18 G	19 E	20 C	21 B	22 H

Part 3

23 C	24 A	25 A	26 C	27 A
28 C	29 B	30 B		

Tapescript

Listening Test 2

This is the Business English Certificate Vantage 2, Listening Test 2.

Part One. Questions 1 to 12.

You will hear three telephone conversations or messages.

Write one or two words or a number in the numbered spaces on the notes or forms below.

After you have listened once, replay each recording.

Conversation One. Questions 1 to 4.

Look at the form below.

You will hear a woman calling about training courses.

You have 15 seconds to read through the form.

[pause]

Now listen, and fill in the spaces.

Man: Good morning, Oakleaf Business Training. How can I help you?
Woman: Hello, my name's Enid Stevens, of Appleyard Smith. I've booked two one-day courses, but now I need to change one of them.
Man: Let me get your details up on the screen. Right, you've booked Report Writing next month . . .
Woman: Yes, that one's OK. It's Taking Minutes that I can't manage, on the eighth of July. Do you know when it's running again?
Man: Let me see. Not until the eighteenth of September, I'm afraid.
Woman: That sounds fine. Oh, I think I'll be abroad then.
Man: Then there's the first and the thirteenth of October.
Woman: I'd like the later date, please.
Man: Fine, I'll change your booking.
Woman: Another thing; it says in your brochure, everyone attending a course gets a certificate, but I haven't received one from a course I took last January.
Man: I'm sorry about that. Which course was it?
Woman: Something to do with dealing with the public . . . ?
Man: That must have been Customer Service.
Woman: Sounds familiar.
Man: OK, I'll put it in the post today.
Woman: Thank you very much. Goodbye.
Man: Goodbye.

[pause]

Now listen to the recording again.

[pause]

Conversation Two. Questions 5 to 8.

Look at the note below.

You will hear a woman ringing about problems with a new telephone system.

You have 15 seconds to read through the note.

[pause]

Now listen, and fill in the spaces.

Man: Hello, Swinburn Telecoms.
Woman: I'd like to speak to Tony Wilson, please.
Man: I'm afraid Tony isn't available. Can I take a message?
Woman: Yes please. I'm Sheila Dallas, from Worldnet.
Man: Right.

appeal. But then someone I met at a training day told me we should use them. His company had used their service for years with no complaints so we followed his advice.

[pause]

Twenty-one

Woman: We'd looked round the market to find the cheapest deal possible but to be honest there wasn't much to choose, in terms of cost, between any of the local suppliers. However, we had a visit from a sales representative from one company and we asked him to make up some complimentary printed letterheads for us. They were exactly what we wanted so that was the deciding factor. I think that personal touch gives a company far better results than advertising ever can.

[pause]

Twenty-two

Man: Obviously there are many different factors to consider when you choose a new supplier. We always used a local company because they were relatively near and we could even pick things up ourselves if necessary. But unfortunately they just became too expensive. Now that express delivery services are widely available, distance is no longer a consideration and we've been able to choose someone who can give us the best package for the lowest cost.

[pause]

Now listen to the recordings again.

[pause]

That is the end of Part Two.

[pause]

Part Three. Questions 23 to 30.

You will hear a radio report about the London stock market.

For each question 23–30, mark one letter (A, B or C) for the correct answer.

After you have listened once, replay the recording.

You have 45 seconds to read through the questions.

[pause]

Now listen, and mark A, B or C.

[pause]

Woman: Hello. I'm Jane Bowen with our regular Friday look at the week just finished on the London stock market.

The general picture is pretty mixed. Shares in the major banks are trading down, while mining companies have surprised analysts with a small rise. Overall, it's been a week of considerable movement, with the highest level reached at the close two days ago and a sharp fall yesterday. A strong recovery saw most of those losses being made up today, but the closing figure still fell short of Wednesday's. Now here's Charles Wrighton with some company news.

Man: Thanks Jane. And first, clothing retailer, Brownlow. Having finally found a buyer for their loss-making sports footwear subsidiary, Hi-form, they've rejected a take-over bid from a leading French retail chain which has been looking to buy into the British market for some time. This activity has moved Brownlow's shares up by twenty per cent to ninety-six pence.

There's a lot of interest in the Lek energy group, which recently bought Westwales Electricity. To the relief of Westwales managers, Lek haven't brought in their own people to run the company. Despite predicted job cuts of something like a third of the engineering staff, no announcement has been made, and indeed, Lek's comprehensive training scheme has been opened to all grades of staff in Westwales. Back to you, Jane.

Woman: We've had a number of emails from investors asking what to do with their shares in gas and electricity companies after their consistently poor performance recently. Many of you might be thinking of getting rid of yours as quickly as possible. But financial experts are fairly optimistic about the outlook for the power sector, and investors may do better to see what happens over the next few months. With so many other investors deciding to cut their losses and sell now, interest in this sector may increase, and that, of course, would push share prices up.

Pharmaceutical companies have done well today. Recently we've seen several periods of rapid expansion in this sector, only for it to be overtaken a short time later by the strong financial institutions. But I actually think the recent performances of pharmaceuticals companies has hidden a steep drop in the share prices of many other companies. All other sectors have lost considerable amounts, but this simply has not been reflected in the overall value of the market, because pharmaceuticals companies are keeping the value high.

Looking next at the sectors whose troubles have been in the news recently: supermarkets, having suffered a downturn in business for over a year, at last have some reason for optimism. The leisure industry, which has suffered even more than supermarkets, is also showing signs of a turnaround. The same cannot be said of the building sector, though, which expects little relief for at least another six months. Charles . . .

Man: One company in the news is Freewaves, which owns a chain in internet cafés. Like other new companies, Freewaves has tended to pay low dividends to investors, preferring to re-invest profits in research and development. Although Freewaves was able to turn in a healthy profit in the first quarter, taking everyone by surprise, the company has now declared operating losses close to a million pounds. This, of course, will make shareholders think about whether to keep their shares.

And news from Simpson's, the big retail group. For years Simpson's have been acquiring other chains, giving them a strong market position, and they now sell everything from make-up to computers. But today Simpson's announced that they are to consolidate their three home improvement chains into one, under the Fresca name.

Woman: Now for the figures . . .

[pause]

Now listen to the recording again.

[pause]

That is the end of Part Three. You now have ten minutes to transfer your answers to your Answer Sheet.

[pause]

Note: Teacher, stop the recording here and time ten minutes. Remind students when there is **one** minute remaining.

That is the end of the test.

Test 3 Reading

Part 1

1 C   2 D   3 A   4 B   5 A   6 B
7 C

Part 2

8 D   9 F   10 C   11 E   12 A

Part 3

13 D   14 B   15 C   16 A   17 B
18 C

Part 4

19 D	20 C	21 A	22 C	23 D
24 C	25 A	26 C	27 A	28 B
29 D	30 A	31 A	32 B	33 B

Part 5

34 TOO   35 CORRECT   36 RESULTS
37 BY   38 CORRECT   39 SO
40 CONCERNING   41 CORRECT
42 ONES   43 THAT   44 ABOUT
45 CORRECT

Test 3 Writing

Part 1

Sample A

Dear colleagues,
As I adviced you in our last meeting, there will be a visit from health and safety inspectors on Monday, 1st April from 9 a.m. until 15 p.m.
The inspection is necessary for our quality management certificate.
Please be prepared for the inspection by telling the staff to tidy up their workplace.
Regards

Band 5

All the content points are successfully addressed, with a controlled, natural use of language, and evidence of a wide range of vocabulary and structure.

Sample B

It was decided that health and safety inspectors would visit our factory to see how it is working. The reason of this inspection is for our staff's safety and health. It is assumed to take about a week. We are expected to give them a certain right to inspect them.

Band 3

The email is reasonably organised and the range of vocabulary and structure is adequate. However, the third content point is not clearly addressed.

senior management about four possible new suppliers.

For each question 23–30, mark one letter (A, B or C) for the correct answer.

After you have listened once, replay the recording.

You have 45 seconds to read through the questions.

[pause]

Now listen, and mark A, B or C.

Woman: As you know, the main supplier of our components announced suddenly last month that they were closing down shortly, leaving us in a very difficult situation. I shortlisted four potential replacement suppliers, and have visited them all. I'll report on each, though I've only found one company that meets our needs entirely.

Initially, I was optimistic about the first company I saw. I was given an enthusiastic welcome and generous hospitality by the MD, but when he took me on a tour of the factory, I began to have a few doubts about his commercial expertise. The factory is enormous – a converted aircraft shed, I think, almost too big to be practical. There is certainly enough machinery to produce the quantities we need, and that, of course, is vital.

However, I had one main concern. The company has recently invested heavily in state-of-the-art production equipment and in a comprehensive training programme for machine operators. But I was surprised to see that half the factory wasn't in use because several important customers had cancelled orders. I was reassured that orders are dispatched quickly, and delivery times are impressive, and distribution isn't a problem – but I'd need to inspect their products more closely to see if the quality's what we require.

The second company looked promising too, because they are based in the region that produces the natural resources to make our components. Everything needed for their activities is available on their doorstep. They have a good working relationship with the local mine owners, who are known to have good safety records. During my visit, the company went into great detail about the quality inspections carried out on the material before it leaves the mines.

This company seemed to have no problems with transport – until I looked more closely. The factory is in a very mountainous region, about six hundred kilometres from the capital city. Passenger flights are fairly frequent, taking under two hours, but the journey by road can take

days. The roads are really inadequate – the whole infrastructure needs massive investment. There is a seaport just over the border with the neighbouring country, which would certainly cut down on distance, but, as far as I can see, it might also bring other problems. We simply can't risk depending on such fragile communications.

The third company I looked at, on the other hand, is on the coast, with good access to the main seaport. Transport and shipping of goods are well organised and, in fact, they own a haulage company as one of their subsidiaries. The production unit is new – built and equipped with the help of investment from the Ministry of Industry. What's more, company workers are involved in decision-making, and industrial relations are excellent. Perfect so far.

Unfortunately, though, their finished products are not of the quality we demand. The specifications are right for our components, so no modifications in design would be necessary. But when I did a quick inspection, I found a higher percentage of faults than we'd be prepared to tolerate. If we chose them, we'd certainly have to negotiate longer warranties than those they're offering at present.

The final company I visited seems to have everything, though. It's ten years old, well established, located between the capital and a major seaport. The company has grown rapidly and has just modernised its factory, thanks to a loan from the World Bank, which has enabled it to install the most up-to-date equipment available on the market. The production unit is now fully automated, and efficiency is the company's great strength.

This company has a well-deserved reputation for the quality of its finished goods. Given their high standard, it's not surprising that the costs are considerable, and they're asking higher prices than the other companies I visited. But I'm confident we'll be able to negotiate on this. The key point in their favour, in my opinion, is their ability to meet deadlines for the duration of a long-term contract. It's easy to meet one deadline, of course – the difficult thing is to do it all the time.

To sum up, then . . .

[pause]

Now listen to the recording again.

[pause]

That is the end of Part Three. You now have ten minutes to transfer your answers to your Answer Sheet.

[pause]

Note: Teacher, stop the recording here and time ten minutes. Remind students when there is **one** minute remaining.

[pause]

That is the end of the test.

Test 4   Reading

Part 1

1 C   2 A   3 B   4 D   5 A   6 B
7 D

Part 2

8 D   9 F   10 B   11 A   12 C

Part 3

13 A   14 A   15 B   16 C   17 C
18 B

Part 4

19 C	20 A	21 B	22 D	23 A
24 B	25 D	26 B	27 A	28 D
29 C	30 A	31 C	32 B	33 D

Part 5

34 FOR   35 CORRECT   36 THE
37 OF   38 WITH   39 CORRECT
40 SUCH   41 CORRECT   42 SO
43 TYPE   44 AROUND   45 IT

Test 4   Writing

Part 1

Sample A

> To: Despatch department
> From: Y. Brown – Manager
> Subject: Failure arrival order client
>
> Dear sir,
>
> According to recent information the ministry of foreign affairs has not received its latest printing order.
> Following details are: one hundred copies of financial statements 2002, please check cause of failure and resend copies as soon as possible.
>
> Kindest regards

Band 5

All the content points are covered, with controlled, natural use of language.

Sample B

> To: Despatch Co-ordinator
> From: Mrs Zoss
>
> Mr Little, who is the manager of River Company, informed me about the order that had not been arrived. He ordered 5000 white paper, 5000 pale grey paper and 1000 envelopes. I think we should get the order ready again and sent it asap.
>
> Thank you

Band 3

All content points are addressed. The range of language is adequate and errors are non-impeding.

Part 2

Sample C

> Dear Sir or Madam
>
> I would like to thank you for your letter, dated 15.5.2003.
> Firstly, unfortunately, we have an international conference on the 10th of June.
> Therefore, this date is not convenient for us. Could you please start at the 11th of June? Furthermore, we would like to know how long the work will take.
>
> Concerning the numbers. The system you announced seems to be difficult. Is there an easier way to handle this problem with different numbers?
>
> As for our further requests, could we have a direct telefon number as well as the name of the person, dealing with us?
>
> We are looking forward to paying the bill as soon as the work is successfully finished in case of any theesing problems.
> We are looking forward to hearing from you.
>
> Yours faithfully,

Band 4

The content points are more than adequately addressed. A range of discourse markers and linking devices is used. Both the register and format are appropriate to the task, and the language is generally accurate.

Sample D

> Dear Mr Young,
>
> Thank for you letter about install new telephone switchboard in our office. But there are some problems we should solved. First, on Tuesday 10 June in our office will take part a celebration of our companys' anniversary. So you can start installation after 10 June in any time you would be able to do it.
> Second, I would like to know how many days' work will be.
> Next, I would like to mention that the system of numbering an extention numbers is to complicated, and I hope that you can suggest me any other way to solve that problem, that you suggesting me now.
> Also, can you tell me the name of your technical representative.
> As you see there are some technical problems with installing new telephone switchboard, and after solving these problems and when the job would be finished we pay for you. Looking forward to hearing from you.
> Yours sincerely,

Band 3
The content points are covered adequately, and the format and register are satisfactory. While the organisation and cohesion are generally satisfactory, there are instances where the reader is not clearly informed.

Test 4   Listening

Part 1

1 DATABASE
2 SUPPLIER
3 HOWARTH
4 IT CO-ORDINATOR
5 (QUALITY) DESIGN
6 EUROPE
7 ADVERTISING CAMPAIGN
8 DISCOUNTS
9 COMMERCIAL HALL
10 380 (SHAREHOLDERS)
11 MICROPHONES
12 AMENDED FIGURES

Part 2

13 D	14 G	15 A	16 E	17 F
18 G	19 B	20 A	21 D	22 C

Part 3

23 C	24 A	25 A	26 C	27 A
28 B	29 B	30 C		

Tapescript

Listening Test 4

This is the Business English Certificate Vantage 2, Listening Test 4.

Part One. Questions 1 to 12.

You will hear three telephone conversations or messages.

Write one or two words or a number in the numbered spaces on the notes or forms below.

After you have listened once, replay each recording.

Conversation One. Questions 1 to 4.

Look at the form below.

You will hear a woman leaving an answerphone message for a company.

You have 15 seconds to read through the notes.

[pause]

Now listen, and fill in the spaces.

Woman: Hello. This is a message for Max Jacobs. It's Alison Gates from Merland Healthcare calling. We're currently working on a website for our healthcare products and we're looking for a company like yours to develop a database for us. The reason I'm contacting you is that I spoke to one of our suppliers and he was very positive about the work you'd done for him.
    I'd be very glad if you could contact me. I'm away all next week but I'll still be able to access my emails – the best thing would be for you to email me at: agates (all one word) at howarth-dot-com. 'Howarth' spelt H-O-W-A-R-T-H, then dot-com.
    If you are interested, the best thing would be for us to meet. It would also be useful for you to talk to our IT co-ordinator at the same time. So if you could indicate your availability over the next few weeks, that'd be good. I look forward to hearing from you. Goodbye.

[pause]

Now listen to the recording again.

[pause]

Conversation Two. Questions 5 to 8.

Look at the notes below.

You will hear a marketing manager reporting on sales of a product.

You have 15 seconds to read through the notes.

[pause]

Now listen, and fill in the spaces.

Man: Mike Shepherd.

Woman: Hello, it's Karen Peterson here, from Marketing. I've been called away on urgent business, but I wanted you to have my report on the MusicMate cassette player to discuss at the Directors' meeting this morning.

Man: Oh, right. OK then, I'd better make a note of this.

Woman: Right. MusicMate has been our second all-time best-seller, with a reputation based on quality design at an inexpensive price.

Man: OK, I've got that.

Woman: Sold originally only on the Asian market, it was then launched in Europe, which rapidly overtook Asia in sales volume, giving us a sure sign that the USA, an even bigger market, should be our next target.

Man: Fine. I don't think we'll be making any decisions about new markets, though.

Woman: OK, back to the UK market then. I think it's important not to neglect our loyal customers here. What would be really helpful would be a new advertising campaign, but I'm aware there's not enough in the budget for that. So I'm suggesting that the way forward is to offer greater discounts – this should form the basis for our marketing plan. That's it. Oh, and, also, any rumours of my department wanting to phase out MusicMate are false. We're very optimistic about its future.

Man: Fine . . . Well look, it's been a pleasure talking . . .

[pause]

Now listen to the recording again.

[pause]

Conversation Three. Questions 9 to 12.

Look at the notes below.

You will hear a woman phoning for information about a meeting.

You have 15 seconds to read through the notes.

[pause]

Now listen, and fill in the spaces.

Woman: Mike, this is Tessa Jones. About the shareholders' meeting on the twenty-fourth.

Man: Yeah.

Woman: The Managing Director says there won't be enough room at the Bankers' Institute.

Man: So what's the alternative?

Woman: We contacted the Commercial Hall – they can take us, but they need the booking immediately. You've got all the details.

Man: OK. What do you need to know?

Woman: First, how much seating should we book?

Man: Well, there are seven hundred and twenty shareholders, but only about half of them ever turn up. So three hundred and eighty chairs would be adequate.

Woman: Mm, what sort of equipment should we ask for?

Man: There'll be five members of the Board on the platform – they'll each need a microphone and we'll also need a couple of OHPs. A video won't be necessary.

Woman: Right, and what about photocopies? I can see to those. What do we need done?

Man: Oh, the agenda – that's essential. The shareholders have already received the annual report, of course, but there were some mistakes in it so we'll need to hand out amended figures at the meeting. I'll let you have those to copy.

Woman: OK. I'll get them done and make sure there are staff available to hand them out. I'll talk to you later.

Man: Fine. Bye.

[pause]

Now listen to the recording again.

[pause]

That is the end of Part One. You now have 20 seconds to check your answers.

[pause]

Part Two. Questions 13 to 22.

Section One. Questions 13 to 17.

You will hear five short recordings.

For each recording, decide which opinion the participant gives about a seminar.

Write one letter (A–H) next to the number of the recording.

Do not use any letter more than once.

Woman: Yes, the middle managers I interviewed commented that they'd like training to cover more specialist areas. To be honest, though, I think they're involved in such a lot of training of new and existing junior staff that they don't fully appreciate the benefits of receiving training themselves.

Man: Mm . . . could be challenging for us then.

Woman: Yes. Whilst welcoming the efforts of senior management, one of the marketing managers I spoke to was quite open about his and his colleagues' views . . . he made the point that there was a widespread feeling that the motivation behind this new programme wasn't clear. They thought it might be used as a way to assess their performance. Because of that, they hadn't been able to make up their minds either way about whether they were in favour.

Man: OK, well, let's think about the content of the programme.

Woman: Right, well we must include sessions on the areas they've actually asked for. Let's have a look . . . customer care and presentation techniques were certainly on their list.

Man: Didn't some of them mention negotiating skills as well?

Woman: OK, let's kick off with what they identified as their priority areas – so we could do presentation techniques this time round and then put forward a proposal for sessions on negotiating skills and customer care and anything else they might want in the future.

Man: That sounds good. We'll go with that.

Woman: We should have more chance like that of fitting in with people's availability.

Man: Well, the company always tried for residential courses at weekends before.

Woman: I gather that wasn't popular. Also, the managers I spoke to weren't keen to come into work even earlier for training sessions.

Man: Mm. Well, if we start off with a series of full-day events during work time, I think that'd be best.

Woman: Yes, sessions early in the morning would be too short – we wouldn't achieve much.

Man: OK, we'll propose that.

Woman: Did you discuss when we'd start?

Man: I suggested March – I'd have liked to get this contract underway before the end of our financial year, and we're already quite booked up from the end of May onwards.

Woman: Don't they have a big launch coming up in the first week of April?

Man: Yes, they said March will be hectic, so as soon as the launch is over and they've had a week to clear up would fit in best.

Woman: OK. So what needs to be done next? Shall we put together a proposed schedule?

Man: Mm, we'll need to do that soon. For now, we've got to get on with devising a survey to go out to everyone included in the programme. We can start working on costings to send to their senior management as soon as we've done that.

Woman: OK, let's just . . .

[pause]

Now listen to the recording again.

[pause]

That is the end of Part Three. You now have ten minutes to transfer your answers to your Answer Sheet.

[pause]

Note: Teacher, stop the recording here and time ten minutes. Remind students when there is **one** minute remaining.

That is the end of the test.

INTERLOCUTOR FRAMES

To facilitate practice for the Speaking test, the scripts followed by the interlocutor for Parts 2 and 3 appear below. They should be used in conjunction with Tests 1–4 Speaking tasks.

Interlocutor frames are not included for Part 1, in which the interlocutor asks the candidates questions directly rather than asking them to perform tasks.

Part 2: Mini presentations (about six minutes)

Interlocutor:
- Now, in this part of the test I'm going to give each of you a choice of three different topics. I'd like you to select one of the topics and give a short presentation on it for about a minute. You will have a minute to prepare this and you can make notes if you want. After you have finished your talk, your partner will ask you a question.
- All right? Here are your topics. Please don't write anything on your topic card.

[Interlocutor hands each candidate a different topic card, and some paper and a pencil for notes. Candidates have one minute's preparation time. Both candidates prepare their talks at the same time, separately.]

Interlocutor:
- All right. Now, *B, which topic have you chosen, A, B or C? Would you like to talk about what you think is important when (xxx). *A, please listen carefully to *B's talk, and then ask him/her a question about it.

[B talks.]

Interlocutor:
- Thank you. Now, *A, please ask *B a question about his/her talk.

[A asks question.]

Interlocutor:
- All right. Now, *A, which topic have you chosen, A, B or C? Would you like to talk about what you think is important when (xxx). *B, please listen carefully to *A's talk, and then ask him/her a question about it.

[A talks.]

Interlocutor:
- Thank you. Now, *B, please ask *A a question about his/her talk.

[B asks question.]

Interlocutor:
- Thank you.

[Materials are collected.]

*USE CANDIDATES' NAMES THROUGHOUT THE TEST.

Part 3: Collaborative task and discussion (about five minutes)

Interlocutor:
- Now, in this part of the test you are going to discuss something together.

[Interlocutor points to the card showing the task while giving the instructions below.]

Interlocutor:
- You have 30 seconds to read the task carefully, and then three minutes to discuss and decide about it together. You should give reasons for your decisions and opinions. You don't need to write anything. Is that clear?

[Interlocutor places the card in front of the candidates.]

Interlocutor:
- I'm just going to listen and then ask you to stop after three minutes. Please speak so that we can hear you.

[Candidates have three minutes to complete the task.]

[Materials are collected.]

[Interlocutor asks one or more of the following questions as appropriate, to extend the discussion.]

Example:
- What other preparations would the company need to make before receiving work experience students? (Why?)
- What are the advantages to a company of offering a work experience programme to business students? (Why?)
- What do you think is the most useful kind of work experience for business students? (Why?)
- What help would you give a student on their first day of work experience? (Why?)
- Which areas of business would you like to have more experience of? (Why?)
- In what ways can businesses develop close links with the community?
- Thank you. That is the end of the Speaking test.

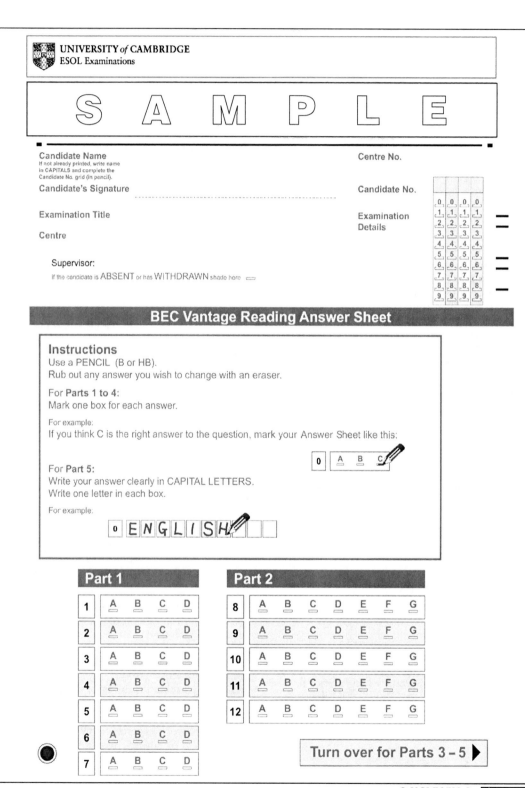

UNIVERSITY *of* CAMBRIDGE
ESOL Examinations

S A M P L E

Candidate Name
If not already printed, write name
in CAPITALS and complete the
Candidate No. grid (in pencil).

Candidate's Signature

Examination Title

Centre

Supervisor:
If the candidate is ABSENT or has WITHDRAWN shade here

Centre No.

Candidate No.

Examination Details

BEC Vantage Reading Answer Sheet

Instructions
Use a PENCIL (B or HB).
Rub out any answer you wish to change with an eraser.

For **Parts 1 to 4**:
Mark one box for each answer.

For example:
If you think C is the right answer to the question, mark your Answer Sheet like this:

0 | A B C D

For **Part 5**:
Write your answer clearly in CAPITAL LETTERS.
Write one letter in each box.

For example:

0 | E N G L I S H

Part 1

1	A B C D
2	A B C D
3	A B C D
4	A B C D
5	A B C D
6	A B C D
7	A B C D

Part 2

8	A B C D E F G
9	A B C D E F G
10	A B C D E F G
11	A B C D E F G
12	A B C D E F G

Turn over for Parts 3 – 5 ▶

Part 3

13	A	B	C	D
14	A	B	C	D
15	A	B	C	D
16	A	B	C	D
17	A	B	C	D
18	A	B	C	D

Part 4

19	A	B	C	D
20	A	B	C	D
21	A	B	C	D
22	A	B	C	D
23	A	B	C	D
24	A	B	C	D
25	A	B	C	D
26	A	B	C	D

27	A	B	C	D
28	A	B	C	D
29	A	B	C	D
30	A	B	C	D
31	A	B	C	D
32	A	B	C	D
33	A	B	C	D

Part 5

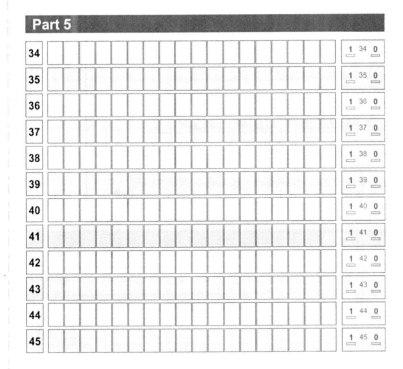

34		1 34 0
35		1 35 0
36		1 36 0
37		1 37 0
38		1 38 0
39		1 39 0
40		1 40 0
41		1 41 0
42		1 42 0
43		1 43 0
44		1 44 0
45		1 45 0

Thanks and acknowledgements

The authors and publishers are grateful to the following for permission to use copyright material in *BEC Vantage 2*. While every effort has been made, it has not been possible to identify the sources of all the material used and in such cases the publishers would welcome information from the copyright owners.

p. 19 For the extract from *Managing People and Activities* by Susan and Barry Curtis, published by Curtis, Pitman 1997 © Pearson Education Limited; p. 22 Extract from 'Developing brand loyalty' by Victoria McKee, *The Sunday Telegraph*, 24 September 2000; p. 39 'Good Listener, Better Manager', p. 59 'How You Should Manage Your Boss', and p. 80 'Sitting in Judgement on Others', reproduced from *Management Today* magazine with the permission of the copyright owner, Haymarket Business Publications Limited; p. 44 Extract from *On the Way Up* by Simon Carne, published by Mercury Business Books, 2000; p. 60 'Sell, sell, sell', with kind permission of John Crace, published in *The Guardian*, 8th February 2000; p. 79 Extract from *Shopping Centre Progress 1999–2000* by Peter Bill, published by the Estates Gazette.

9 780521 5445